Travel Tips
for Teachers

Other books in this series include:

Financial Tips for Teachers by Alan Jay Weiss and Larry Strauss

Travel Tips for Teachers

Sunni Bloyd

Willowisp Press
Worthington, Ohio

Published by Willowisp Press, Inc.
401 E. Wilson Bridge Road, Worthington, Ohio 43085
Copyright © 1990 by RGA Publishing Group, Inc.

Printed in the United States of America
10 9 8 7 6 5 4 3 2 1
ISBN: 0-87406-467-8

Cover photograph of French Polynesia and the Eiffel Tower
courtesy of the French Government Tourist Office. Photograph
of Big Ben courtesy of the British Tourist Authority.

Contents

Acknowledgments

The author would like to express appreciation for the continuing affection and support of the staff and faculty of Hanau American School (Department of Defense Dependent School, Hanau, West Germany), and of the Yorba and Cerro Villa middle schools (both of Orange Unified School District, Orange, California), especially Cheryl Stephens, Karen Gordon, and Cathy Jennings.

This book would not have been possible without the assistance and information provided by many people who shared their special experience and knowledge. Thanks go to Maureen Rosen, Compass Travel; Teachers Tax Service; Department of Defense Dependent Schools; the Federal Department of Education, Division of International Education; Loralee Heckler, TSA Travel; John Jensen, Campus Travel Services; Harwood Tours; Lakeland Tours; TSA Special Services; Joyce Krauser; Evelyn Busse; Douglas Mann; Wanda Smith; Karen Verostek; Debbie Gillen; Tye Roy; Joann Beard; Lynn Tubbe; Mrs. Gressa Basey, U.S. Office of Education; NEA Special Services; U.S. Passport Agency, Los Angeles; U.S. Customs Service, Los Angeles; FTA Special Services; Linda Fuller; Christine and Michael Gill; and my editor, Margaret Shumate.

Preface

This book is written expressly for teachers who would like to travel more but have somehow never gotten around to it. It's intended to open doors, to show you how valuable travel can be, both professionally and personally. By reading *Travel Tips for Teachers,* you should become familiar with some opportunities you might not have been aware of, and gain enough information to take advantage of them.

Travel Tips for Teachers contains sections on all sorts of travel that teachers might find particularly interesting. It's packed with special tips garnered from the author's twenty years of experience living and teaching all around the world. In addition, it includes the addresses and telephone numbers of a myriad of resources helpful to a teacher planning to travel, work, or study abroad.

Because this work is written for teachers, who often must make do on a limited budget, it contains a great deal of information about bargains—free or discount tickets, books, accommodations, and so forth. Much of the free material (for example, the pamphlets offered by state and national tourist offices) has the additional value of being ideal for use in the classroom.

While all the offers and rates mentioned in this book are valid at the time of this writing, special offers and bargain rates have a habit of changing overnight. The specific prices and fees mentioned here should therefore be considered as guidelines rather than absolutes. Check with the distributor or booking agent before you make final plans.

For similar reasons the tax information presented in *Travel Tips for Teachers* should not be used in lieu of professional legal or accounting advice. It is designed to acquaint you with the provisions and interpretations of the Internal Revenue Code that pertain to your profession.

Just as the best classroom instruction usually begins with a lesson plan, so the best trips begin with a travel plan. Here, gathered together for you into one convenient book, is the information you need to turn your travel dreams into wonderful experiences.

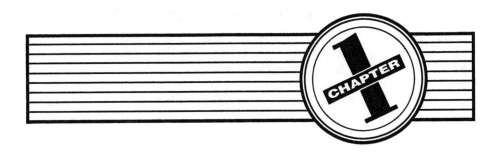

CHAPTER 1

Doing Your Homework

There's a world of travel just waiting for teachers! Weekend ski trips, a cruise to the Bahamas during spring break, summer vacation in the Far East, even a year in Europe—there's no limit to the opportunities open to you. Educators can take advantage of fantastic bargains and great exchange programs designed just for them, as well as great deals on package tours and last-minute fares.

Whatever U.S. sights or foreign climes you dream of visiting, now's the moment to turn those dreams into reality. This book can help you turn wishes into action. But before you fly, you've got to go to ground school. Doing a little homework will help you to make flight plans that will assure you of clear skies and happy landings.

Educators can take advantage of fantastic bargains.

GREAT EXPECTATIONS

Perhaps you already know exactly where you want to go on your vacation. But if all you have is a hazy idea, what should you do to turn that vague feeling into solid plans?

11

What Are You Looking For?

What, exactly, should this particular trip do for you?

The first leg of your journey is to find out what you're expecting from a trip. It's all too easy to come back from a vacation feeling as though you'd never gone away, simply because you didn't plan your trip to meet your needs. What, exactly, should this particular trip do for you?

Rest and Relaxation

Sometimes you need to unwind. If it's the end of a hard year and you want some quiet time to recoup, don't plan a strenuous trip. Even though you normally enjoy cross-country driving, maybe this is the year to take the train or bask in the sun at a lakeside condo a mere hour from home.

Physical Invigoration

On the other hand, maybe you need to work up a sweat to wash away the cobwebs after a few months in the classroom. If so, you could select destinations or travel packages that offer plenty of exercise. There are tours that offer everything from lobbing a few over the tennis nets at Wimbledon to whitewater rafting down the Colorado River.

Aesthetic Experience

Some trips provide spiritual refreshment without physical exertion. Viewing the wonders of nature—whether it's the sunrise at the edge of the Grand Canyon or the stars twinkling over Waikiki—can wash away the petty irritations of life by putting them into perspective.

Entertainment

What better time to enjoy yourself than while on a vacation? Cast aside the work ethic and indulge yourself. It's easy to find a spot that caters to the need for entertainment. Just look for someplace that provides a variety of activities and events, as well as a staff whose only job is to pamper you. Then let go—and have a ball.

Educational and Cultural Enrichment

You may decide to view your vacation as an opportunity to learn something new or to experience first-hand something you've only read about. Do you want to improve your knowledge of French culture or of the Brazilian rain forest? Would you love to visit the NASA Space Center? You may want to give yourself a fresh look at a subject you've been teaching, and perhaps bring back souvenirs that will make the topic come alive for your students.

Foreign travel can fill your need for intellectual adventure admirably. Visiting museums, meeting people from different cultures, and reliving history can broaden your perspective on life. Contrary to what you may think, it's not necessary to spend a fortune for educational or cultural enrichment, whether in the U.S. or Europe. Escorting a student tour to Washington, D.C. or working overseas costs virtually nothing and can be immensely rewarding.

Experience first-hand something you've only read about.

Adventure

There's a little bit of Marco Polo in all of us. You may want your vacation to include the unusual, the daring, and the exciting . . . with perhaps an element of fantasy thrown in for seasoning. Just how daring an adventure ought to be depends on the adventurer. For some, camping out at Yellowstone is adventure enough. For others, a visit to the bazaar at Marrakesh, with its exotic sights, sounds, and smells, will satisfy the adventuresome urge. Yet others want to hike through a rain forest or sit beside gorillas on an African hillside.

Escape

Getting away from it all appeals to many people. Change—of setting, pace, or routine—is the main ingredient in any vacation. A few days in a totally different world can bring you back refreshed and ready to tackle the problems of life in the classroom with new inspiration.

Change—of setting, pace, or routine—is the main ingredient in any vacation.

Togetherness

Taking a trip with your family is a good way to grow closer and to get to know one another better. The family vacation can be a time to develop the ties between parent and child, to share special interests and activities, and to encourage the skills of independent thinking and self-expression in your child.

Class outings give you the same opportunity to get to know your students. Besides the educational benefits of participating in a choir competition, visiting the local art museum, or attending a leadership conference, taking a trip releases both student and teacher from some of the restraints of the classroom. You have more time to dry a tear, laugh at a joke, or share a sandwich. Discussions aren't limited to what's on the lesson plan. Sharing the joy of winning the biggest trophy at the meet or the disappointment of coming home empty-handed creates an emotional bond that enriches both the classroom experience and your life.

Visiting Friends or Relatives

For many people, a vacation is the time to renew ties with family and friends. Visit Aunt Minnie or your college roommate, let your dad measure the kids on the same closet door that holds faded penciled notations of your height, or reminisce over old times at your high school reunion. You'll come home refreshed and energized after strengthening your emotional ties with the past.

Matching Your Personality to Your Vacation

Travel agents claim that every cruise or tour has its own individual personality, so they try to find out about their clients' likes, dislikes, and hobbies in order to match them with the perfect vacation. You can do the same thing for yourself by considering the following questions.

Are You an Outdoor or an Indoor Person?

If archaeology excites you, you might want to sign on as a volunteer archaeologist in Israel for the summer.

Someone who loves the outdoors will probably prefer a vacation that involves camping, hiking, riding, hunting, fishing, or boating. A person who prefers the indoors, on the other hand, may be interested in nice accommodations, in educational, social, or cultural opportunities, and in having someone else do the cooking!

What Do You Like to Do?

If archaeology excites you, you might want to sign on as a volunteer archaeologist in Israel for the summer. If all you're up to doing by the end of the school year is lying in the sun, you ought to book a do-nothing week in Acapulco. Cruise lines offer a number of theme cruises centered around such interests as magic, sports, and solving mysteries.

Do You Love History and Museums?

If the answer is yes, you may want to try a tour vacation. Everything is arranged for you, and knowledgeable guides make sure that you don't miss anything. (Note that many universities offer good tours for college credit.) You could select a package tour and travel with a group, or a day tour, where you join a group for only one day to see specific attractions.

Many universities offer good tours for college credit.

How Do You Like to Dress on Vacation?

The options range from fancy-dress cruises and posh European casinos to nudist camps in Spain. You won't enjoy yourself if you feel overdressed or underdressed while you're trying to have fun. Some countries—especially those in the Middle East—frown upon women wearing shorts. Look into what's expected of you before you make your reservations to be sure you'll be comfortable.

Some countries frown upon women wearing shorts.

Do You Like Keeping Control of Things?

If you don't like to have other people telling you what to do, a tour is not for you. Independent travel, where you can make your own schedule, will suit you best.

What Did You Do on Your Last Vacation?

Your past vacations are good indicators of what you do and do not enjoy, and they've given you a set of expectations by which you'll judge any future trips. If your last journey was a full tour of Egypt, including floating down the Nile on a barge, a weekend trip to even the best Egyptian museum here in the States will pale in comparison.

Finally, ask yourself some personal questions. In general, what kind of a person are you? Are you a quiet reader or television watcher, or a high-energy doer who always has to be on the go? Is your family close-knit, with members sharing many activities, or does everybody go his or her separate way? Does having your children (or a whole busload of students) close to you for an entire trip sound like heaven, or will they get on your nerves after the first hour? Tailor your plans to fit your own comfort.

RESEARCHING THE POSSIBILITIES

By now, you ought to have a pretty good idea of what you want your trip to do for you. All you have to do is match travel plans with your expectations. Research is a crucial ingredient in successful planning, and now is the time to use those research skills you've been teaching your students. Before making your final decision, ferret out as many options as you can.

Other Teachers

Your colleagues are excellent resources. Nearly every faculty has a few teachers who have participated in exchange programs, biked through Canada, hiked through the Great American Northwest, or shepherded 120 eighth-graders through the nation's capital. Ask about their experiences—the high points, the trials and tribulations—and about expenses. Does it sound like something you'd want to do?

At Work

Fliers offering unique opportunities for educators flutter into the teachers' lounge around Easter. Check the bulletin boards for special offers on tours and circulars seeking teachers to chaperone foreign students visiting the U.S. during the summer. Look carefully at the "junk" mail that comes into your school mailbox. A conference, a course offered in your teaching area, or a summer-employment advertisement could be a magic carpet to places you've always wanted to visit—and the ride may be tax-deductible!

At Home

Watch your mail for special offerings from NEA or

AFT, your state teachers' association, and other teachers' groups. Associations such as the Smithsonian, National Geographic, or your university alumni association also regularly offer many trips and educational travel opportunities that appeal to teachers.

Required Reading

Read up on the subject. Your newspaper's travel section will give you a good idea of some places you may have never considered visiting. Browse through the entertainment section to find out what kinds of cruises and package deals are available. Read the fine print—prices, amenities, and options—very carefully so that you'll understand what each travel package offers and can compare it with others.

Check the magazine racks for travel magazines. These cover the latest seasonal travel hot spots, and they run plenty of advertisements for cruises and tours. Even if you eventually decide against all the tours and trips you've read about, you will have gained valuable insight into the kind of travel you seek.

Drop by the library or browse in the nearest bookstore. You will find an amazing array of different kinds of travel literature, with books about hundreds of destinations aimed at all kinds of travelers. Just reading the titles alone will give you new ideas, and a quick glance through a book's table of contents will tell you if it's worth taking home.

Books Worth Owning

Some books are just too good to have to return to the library. Several sorts of travel guides can help you plan your trip, while other books should have a permanent place in your suitcase. (See Appendix 1 for a list of absolutely indispensable books.)

See Appendix 1 for a list of absolutely indispensable books.

There are three sorts of guides to world travel: cultural/tourist guides, accommodations/restaurant guides, and all-around guides. The *Michelin Green Guides* and *Baedaker's Guides* are topnotch cultural travel books. They offer complete information on the history, culture, and points of interest of many countries and individual cities. Small but accurate city maps and explanations of public transportation in major cities make this type of guide indispensable if you are planning a self-guided tour.

Before you leave the United States, purchase one of these guides for each area you intend to visit. They are not available in most tourist centers, and the standard tourist books sold in street corner stalls are often inferior.

While they may not be much help to you at this stage of planning your trip, accommodation guides can be invaluable once you start to map out an itinerary. Accommodation guides can be found to cover nearly every sort of place to stay. The *Michelin Red Guides* (which list accommodations only) provide information on all hotels, inns, and pensions; *Camping Europe* gives complete information on hundreds of campgrounds; and listings of inexpensive bed-and-breakfast accommodations are available from national tourist offices.

Add 15 percent to prices quoted in travel books for every year after the copyright date.

Other guides, such as the *Let's Go* series, *Fodor's Guides,* and *Frommer's Guides* cover accommodations and restaurants as well as sights to see, and provide a good overview of the country for browsers seeking a destination. They're ideal for footloose folks who want to go as the spirit moves them because they recommend places to stay or dine.

A good travel book can give you a detailed account of the sights to see, places to stay, and restaurants where you can ruin your waistline! Remember, however, that the prices quoted in travel books are at least a year old, so add about 15 percent for every year after the copyright dates.

Freebies

These special offers are just too good to waste:

Maps of Europe/North America

Up-to-date maps can help you plan your trip. For a free travel guide featuring color maps of North America or Europe, write to Best Western International, P.O. Box 1023, Phoenix, AZ 85064-0203. Request either the *North America Travel Guide* (which contains maps of the United States, the Caribbean, Canada, and Mexico) or the *European Travel Guide* with color maps of 14 European countries.

Museum Guide

For those who are museum freaks, the European Travel Commission publishes a free guide to more than 100 of Europe's leading museums. If you've always wanted to see "Winged Victory," it pays to know that she's in the Louvre in Paris. Museums in twenty-three countries—everywhere from Iceland to Yugoslavia—are described. Send a stamped, self-addressed envelope along with your request to the European Travel Commission, 630 Fifth Avenue, Suite 610, New York, NY 10111.

Free guide to more than 100 of Europe's leading museums.

Tourist Offices

Most countries, all the fifty states, and many large cities publish brochures, pamphlets, and booklets for tourists. Most foreign countries maintain tourist offices in the United States (a list of the major tourist offices and their addresses can be found at the back of this book). Although the quality of such offerings varies, by asking for specific information you can obtain descriptions of the major tourist attractions, listings of accommodations, and even maps, for little or no cost.

Travel Agents

If you explain what you're looking for in a vacation, a good travel agent can come up with several possibilities. Travel agents have usually traveled extensively and can give you firsthand information. Naturally, any travel agent you talk to will want to sell you something—usually a cruise or tour, since that's the stock-in-trade of many agencies—but you don't need to feel pressured to buy right away. Drop by several travel agencies if you have time and make a note of anyone who seems especially helpful. You'll probably want assistance later in making reservations and finding accommodations.

CHOOSING YOUR DESTINATION

By this time you probably have five or six possible trips in mind. Sit down for a few moments and go through all the information you have. If you will be traveling with family or friends, discuss all of the possibilities with them. Then choose the vacation that appeals to you the most.

Review your choice to make certain that it's really the best solution for you. The following questions can help.

---

1. Does the vacation you've chosen meet most of your expectations?

2. Is it suitable in terms of what you can and can't do, physically, emotionally, and financially?

3. Is the pace right for you—neither too slow nor too hectic?

4. Are your plans flexible enough to allow you to have a good time even if things go wrong?

5. Do you feel *good* about your choice?

Asking yourself these questions will help you to evaluate your plans and adapt them to correct any minor problems. And there will, of course, be minor problems. What trip is free of them? You may have to make a few changes, but the time and effort you have been putting into making good decisions will surely pay off in a trip well worth remembering—a wonderful holiday designed specifically for you.

BALANCING TIME AND MONEY

You've made the big decision. Now you know where you want to go. All that's left is to tidy up the loose ends and arrange the 1,001 details that will take you from decision to action. It's time to bring your travel plans into the realm of reality by looking at two factors that play a role in *any* decision: the time you have to spend, and the money you can afford to part with.

How Much Time Can You Take, and When?

The Teacher's Calendar
Unless you're prepared to take a sabbatical or retire,

the time you have for traveling is limited by the school calendar. The big chunks of time are probably winter holidays, spring break, and summer vacation. But don't forget about the three- and four-day holidays. You can fly down to Cancun over Memorial Day weekend, or skip off to Aspen for Presidents' Day weekend. If turkey is nothing but a big bore to you, take a cruise over Thanksgiving.

Tailor your plans to the time you have available. What is appropriate to the season you have in mind for your trip? If you can get away in December, think about cruises to warmer weather or ski trips to Colorado or the Swiss Alps.

Know when *not* to go. Being in a foreign country on what is a national or religious holiday there can be disappointing (in Holland, for example, museums and shops are closed for the queen's birthday). Practically all tourist activity and public transportation halt on Christmas and Easter in European countries, so all but the simplest kind of sightseeing is out of the question at those times.

Know when not *to go.*

Consider how conditions will affect you. If you can't stand crowds, don't visit New Orleans near Mardi Gras time. If heat and dust do you in, take your trips in the winter or spring.

How long can you be gone? Longer trips should be planned for summer or semester breaks so that you'll have ample time to rest upon your return. You don't want to walk into the classroom Monday morning with jet lag. Also, don't try to see and do too much on one trip. If you try to see Asia in twelve days, all you'll remember is a blur. Concentrate on one or two countries, and you'll gain a much better understanding of the culture and history of the area without that "If this is Monday, I must be in Hong Kong" confusion that afflicts many tourists.

Finding More Time for Travel

Think creatively about how much time you have for travel. Most teachers have three or more "any purpose" leave days a year. While some school systems do not allow teachers to combine these with holidays, others are more reasonable. Ask your principal or union representative what your school system's policy is. If you apply well in advance, you may be able to leave early over Christmas break or stretch Thanksgiving into a week.

Faculty members who have been with their school district for some time can apply for sabbatical leave (leave without pay) for as long as three years. You can travel, study, or work overseas and return to your old job, although you probably won't be guaranteed the same school. While some districts allow sabbatical leave only for teachers who are working on a higher degree, districts with declining enrollment are often glad to give an unpaid vacation to a teacher who is toward the top of the pay scale.

"Seasons"—High, Low, and In Between

Occasionally time *is* money. Such is the case with airfares and resort accommodations. The amount that you will be charged for your hotel room or airplane ticket is figured according to three schedules, known as "seasons." You've probably heard of "low season" and "high season," but the "shoulder season" may be unfamiliar to you.

Simply put, you will pay the highest prices during high season, which is the most popular time to visit a tourist spot, take a cruise, or fly the friendly skies. Low season is the least popular time to visit, and the shoulder is the intermediate weeks (often in May and October) when tourist numbers are declining. You will pay more for accommodations and transportation in high season than in shoulder or low season, even if you stay in the same room.

The exact dates of high, shoulder, and low seasons vary with the location and attractions of a particular destination. During the winter, rates are high at ski resorts and tropical getaway islands. During the summer, vacationers will pay premium prices to visit lake or ocean resorts and amusement parks. Airplane fares peak during the Christmas and Easter holidays and over summer vacation, just when teachers are free to travel.

Check the high, low, and shoulder seasons of the places you wish to visit, and be aware of them when you comparison shop. If at all possible, try to select vacations that will be on low- or shoulder-season rates.

Because as a teacher you must take your vacations during school holidays, you may not be able to escape paying high-season rates for standard travel packages. And if you are determined to visit a particular place at a particular time, you may just have to pay the higher rate (after all, there's no point in visiting a ski resort in the middle of summer!).

How Much Can You Spend?

The amount of money you have to spend is important. Obviously, there is a major cost difference between a trip to Disneyland and a trip around the world. Your financial limits will set the boundaries on where you can go, and for how long.

However, by being flexible about the quality of accommodations you will accept (for example, a bed-and-breakfast instead of a four-star hotel), you can keep expenses under control. Other options suitable for school holidays—such as camping, hiking, bicycling, exchanging homes, or staying at farms—bring travel into reach for those with even the slimmest pocketbooks.

While it seems that the cost of any trip always expands to consume the available amount of money plus an uncomfortable bit more, when you plan carefully and reasonably for expenses, you will avoid coming home to a stack of credit card bills.

Before you commit yourself to any independent trip, tour, or cruise take a hard look at the total cost. What expenses, if any, might accrue in addition to the costs of transportation, accommodation, and meals? Are there optional trips you will want to take? Is there anyone you would be expected to tip? Take into consideration all airport taxes, visa fees, tolls, and luggage transfer costs.

Sit down with a pencil and paper and figure out what you will be spending, taking all of the above into consideration. Then add between $100 and $150 a day for souvenirs, gifts, taxis, telephone calls, film, admission fees, snacks, bargains, and walking-around money. If this figure seems too high, come up with your own mad-money estimate, but keep in mind that it should be about equal to what you plan to pay for your accommodations and food combined.

If your trip suddenly seems too expensive, a simple way of cutting costs is to cut the length of the trip.

Add about $100 a day to your budget for souvenirs, gifts, and so on.

This may involve leaving out a side trip or two, but at least you'll still get to go.

Financial Assistance

A shortage of funds is no barrier to travel for a resourceful teacher. Check out scholarships for foreign study, overseas employment, and programs that offer teachers free passage in exchange for chaperoning student groups. (See chapters 5 and 6 for more information on traveling with student groups and finding jobs overseas.)

The National Endowment for the Humanities pays for teachers to take time off to do research, a respite that can be as long as a year or as short as a summer vacation. It also offers other programs for secondary teachers. For the free pamphlet *Introduction to Programs,* write to: National Endowment for the Humanities, Washington, D.C. 20506.

The Institute of International Education (IIE) puts out two publications that may contain the solution to your financial dilemma. *Fulbright and Other Grants for Graduate Study* and *Financial Resources for International Study* contain information about grants offered by the U.S. and foreign governments, and they direct the reader to other publications listing grants available both here and abroad. Both are free. Write to: IIE, 809 United Nations Plaza, New York, NY 10017. (Remember that the U.S. government now considers grants to be taxable income, with the exception of what you actually spend on tuition, books, and educational materials.)

WHY YOU NEED A TRAVEL AGENT

Travel agents do not usually charge you for their services.

Some people have an unreasonable resistance to using a travel agent. They will spend hours on the phone on hold, waiting for an airline booking agent to tell them what flights are available, when they could be sitting in a travel agent's office by a nice potted palm, leafing through travel brochures and watching the travel agent do all the work!

The unvarnished truth is that even if you're willing to collect reams of airline schedules in search of the absolute *lowest* fare, a good travel agent can save you money on almost any type of trip. Do not be put off by the attractive office (or the potted palm)— *you* aren't paying the rent. Travel agents do not usually charge you for their services, unless you want something that involves transatlantic cables or international telephone calls. Instead, they receive commissions from carriers, hotels, tour operators, and motorcoach companies when they sell tickets.

Reputable travel agents have professional training, experience, and expertise. It's their job to pull together all the elements of your trip— transportation, itinerary, accommodations, and sightseeing—into a harmonious whole. They may do this by booking each element separately to create a custom-designed tour, known as Foreign Independent Travel (FIT). FIT is expensive, but it does offer flexibility and independence. Or they may make arrangements with a tour operator who can offer the perfect package for you. A tour has the advantage of being cheaper, because the tour company can get better prices on accommodations and travel by buying blocks of tickets.

The Advantages of a Travel Agency

There are several advantages of working with a travel agency. First, travel agents have access to the schedules of many airlines through the computer that graces nearly every desk in the agency's office. A good agent can quickly weed through the ever-changing thicket of fares and flights to find you the best deal, *if you request the lowest price.*

If you're searching for the cheapest fare (through a charter company, for example), you'll find a travel agent to be invaluable. Charter companies are not usually listed on the computer, and the agent must use the telephone. The lines are always busy, and it's a lot more pleasant for you to have the travel agent wait on hold in your stead!

A travel agent can save you money in other ways. Many types of tours and cruises—often the cheapest ones—are available *only* through travel agents. Travel agents also have books that list all the accommodations in a given area. How better to find the best rooms at the lowest price?

Travel agents sometimes offer trip-cancellation insurance.

A final reason to go to a travel agent: many offer low-cost trip-cancellation insurance. Some even provide it automatically with your ticket.

Selecting a Travel Agent

ASTA

You can tell whether your travel agent is a professional by the organizations he or she works with. Membership in the American Society of Travel Agents, for example, means that the travel agency ascribes to a strict code of ethics. If the agency has approval from the Air Traffic Conference, it has met stringent financial requirements and is allowed to issue domestic airline tickets. It has met similar standards if it has approval from the International Air Transport Association (IATA) and can write tickets on international airlines.

When your travel agent displays the initials "CTC" (which stand for "Certified Travel Counselor") after his or her name, it means that he or she has had at least five years of experience in the business and two years of additional training. While this doesn't mean that agents who do not have the initials after their names aren't good travel agents, the certified travel counselor can usually be depended upon to handle your case with professionalism.

The best way to choose a travel agent is to visit a few. Inquire at the Better Business Bureau if you have any doubts, and settle upon one who seems to suit your style.

Your Teachers' Union as a Travel Agent

Your teachers' union—on both the local and national levels—may offer many of the services you would find at a travel agency. In some states, notably California, you can make individual travel arrangements through the special-services division of your state teachers' association. Other states offer far less, choosing to concentrate on obtaining discounts on tours and cruises, accommodations, entertainment, tours, and so forth. (Benefits obtained through teachers' unions are described in chapter 3.)

What a Travel Agent Should Do For You

- Act in your best interests to find a vacation that's inexpensive for the quality it provides.

- Select reliable tour and cruise operators.

- Sell you travel and health insurance suited to your trip.

- Advise you honestly on money-saving opportunities, such as charter trips.

- Inform you about current trends in the industry—what's popular, and what's a good buy.

- Help you select a vacation package that suits you.

- Deal with you ethically.

- Advise you on what to expect on your trip.

- Prepare a detailed itinerary of your trip.

- Make reservations, order tickets, make special arrangements, and tell you exactly how much everything will cost.

- Fight on your side if you run into problems with a tour company, hotel, or airline.

- Refund your money quickly if you have to cancel.

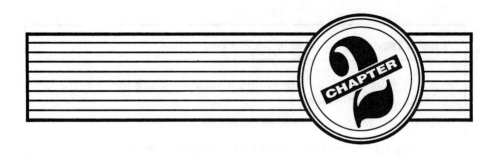

CHAPTER 2

What's Out There

You've now sifted through the travel brochures, asked your friends and relations for their recommendations, and put yourself in the hands of a travel agent who can guide your dreams to fruition. You know where you want to go—but how do you get there, and where do you hang your hat? The options are infinite.

TRANSPORTATION

There are other ways to travel than by automobile or airplane.

On some trips, the choice of transportation is automatic. If you're taking the kids out to visit Uncle Henry on the farm, it's the family car or van. If you're trying to wedge in a hurry-up trip to Australia at the end of the summer, it's obviously a plane. But all too often we choose a mode of transportation without thinking about the difference it makes to the trip. There *are* other ways to travel than by automobile or airplane, and the decision to use one of them represents a different outlook on the trip itself.

Up in the Air

Until you can cash in those reservations for a rocket-ship trip to the moon, the quickest mode of travel is the airplane. You hand over your luggage at one end, relax in a (more-or-less) comfortable seat for anywhere from a few minutes to a few hours, then disembark and pick up your luggage at the other end. While you may visit with your neighbor or look out of your window occasionally when the pilot calls your attention to some geographical feature, on the whole it's an uninvolved trip. Its only purpose is to get you from point A to point B—period.

When the Means Becomes the End

Trains, tour buses, ships, and even recreational vehicles change the whole complexion of a trip, because the journey itself becomes an important part of the vacation. Because the trip usually takes much longer than it would by plane, you have more of an opportunity to make friends with fellow travelers in adjoining seats or compartments of a train, ship, or bus. And the folks in the big rig next to your R.V. might turn out to be people you met last year in Montreal. Sitting by a big window on a leisurely bus or train trip, you can peek into the lives of people in rural America or big-city France. The porthole on a cruise liner may reveal swooping seagulls and an ocean surface polka-dotted with pink jellyfish. Think about all of the options before you choose your mode of transportation.

The journey becomes part of the vacation.

One if by Land . . .

Some form of ground transportation is always necessary, whether you're taking a bus to get to the airport or going on a safari across the Sahara by Jeep.

Automobiles

Old Henry Ford did the traveling public a favor when he popularized the automobile. Eighty percent of all vacationers in the United States travel by car.

Some automobile and bus trips share the same

characteristics as plane travel. Anyone who's ever ridden from Oklahoma to California in a hurry can't tell you much about the scenery, and they probably aren't too fond of their means of conveyance by the time they reach their destination.

Such unleisurely trips aside, automobile aficionados tout the freedom to stop as often as one likes or to press on further than originally planned. Drivers can pack a car with enough baggage to make a telephone-booth-stuffing fraternity brother green with envy. If you aren't comfortable setting out on a trip without at least three suitcases, a picnic lunch, and a few pillows for the kids in back, the automobile is your mode of travel.

On the other hand, getting lost in a strange city is not the happiest experience, and those who are accustomed to quiet rural routes may have some problem adjusting to busy freeways.

Overseas, the problem can be compounded by cultural differences. In some countries, such as England and Singapore, cars use the "wrong" side of the road, a situation that takes a little getting used to. Negotiating a German autobahn or a Parisan traffic circle requires quick reflexes and a certain amount of daredevil in one's makeup. Such challenges disconcert some drivers. For them, spending hours behind the steering wheel or poring over a road map is no vacation.

Renting a car in Europe.

If you'd like to have the freedom of driving once you've arrived at your destination by some other means of transportation, why not rent a car? This makes good sense if you're planning a meandering trip through Europe. You can save $600 or more on car rental in Europe by making arrangements in advance from the U.S. For more information, contact Foremost Eurocar, 5430 Van Nuys Blvd., Van Nuys, CA 91401, 800-423-3111 (800-272-3299 in California); Auto Europe, P.O. Box 500, Yorktown Heights, NY 10598, 800-223-5555; or Cortel International, 800-228-2535.

If you want to drive but don't have a car, Auto Driveaway Company has the solution to your transportation woes—in this hemisphere, anyway. Travelers over twenty-one with valid driver's licenses can help Auto Driveaway deliver cars to cities all over

North America. When you drive one of their late-model cars, you get free use of the automobile (no rental or mileage charges), a free tank of gas, maps and routings, and car insurance. All you have to do is pay part of the gas and drive the car. Contact Auto Driveaway Co., 310 South Michigan Ave., Chicago, IL 60604, 800-346-2277. Auto Movers (800-732-1541) and A-1 Movers (800-247-1301) offer similar deals.

Recreational Vehicles

It used to be that people with a hankering to camp out on a driving trip took along a pup tent and a Coleman stove. Today, with the advent of the recreational vehicle, they can take along everything—*including* the kitchen sink, the microwave, the television set, and a couple of lawn chairs. With a motor home or trailer, you can keep your independence. You can visit family or friends and still sleep in your own bed every night. Or, you can join an R.V. club and make regular outings to destinations far and wide.

Buying a trailer or motor home is a big investment. Because an R.V. can easily cost $35,000, even the most avid R.V.'ers recommend renting one to start with. Rental agencies can be found all over the country. *The R.V. Directory,* which lists 100 dealers and provides information about costs and the availability of rentals, can be purchased for about four dollars from the Recreational Vehicle Association of North America, Suite 500, 3251 Old Lee Highway, Fairfax, VA 22030, 800-336-0355.

Renting an R.V.— in the U.S. or Europe.

In Europe, you could solve two problems—where to stay and how to get around—by renting an R.V. Auto Europe offers motor homes and campers for lease in seven European countries. Prices for a wide variety of rigs start as low as $225 a week (with no mileage charge). The firm operates a reception center with shopping, currency exchange, laundry facilities, and available storage for extra luggage. More information is available through your travel agent or Auto Europe at the toll-free number previously listed. Share-A-Ride, Inc., 61 Studiestrasse, 1554 Copenhagen V., Denmark also lets you carry your lodging with you. Rental rates begin at $150 a week. Pick up your vehicle in any of nine European countries. Guides to 4,000 campgrounds are furnished with the rental. If you'd like to know more about renting (or buying) vans and campers in Europe, order the $5.95 guide *Europe Free—The Car, Van and R.V. Travel Guide* from Shore/Campbell Publications, 1437 Lucile Ave., Los Angeles, CA 90026.

Trains

Nearly every country in the world has a passable rail system, and most of them offer some form of discount rates to tourists. Eurail is the most famous, but not the only discounted rail travel opportunity.

A Eurail Pass must be purchased before you leave the United States.

The Eurail Pass, like many other discount rail tickets, must be purchased before you leave the United States. You will receive a ticket about the size of a credit card, which identifies you as a Eurail Pass holder and states the duration of the pass, which can vary from fifteen days to three months. Don't worry about the Eurail Pass expiring before you get to use it. The ticket agent will stamp the date on your pass the first time you use it, and your allotted time will begin then.

Buying one of these passes is a great way to see the world, as long as you don't mind hoisting your own luggage and occasionally trying to sleep next to a snoring stranger.

Cars (and fares) are separated into first and second class, and smoking and nonsmoking. Be sure you have the correct ticket for the car in which you are riding. First-class travel is advised during the holidays because second-class compartments will be crowded. Make seat reservations through the rail-ticket office in advance of your departure. (There will be a small fee for the reservation.)

Specific information can be obtained from *Eurail Guide,* by Kathryn Saltzman Turpin and Marvin L. Saltzman, an annually updated guide to rail travel in 114 countries. This thorough book lists discounted rail-travel options worldwide. It's published by Eurail Guide Annual, 27540 Pacific Coast Highway, Malibu, CA 90265.

Order European railway timetables.

If you wish to plan your departures down to the minute, order European railway timetables and *Eurail Travelers Guide* (which comes complete with a foldout map of the European rail system, along with information on discounts and reduced-fare bonuses) from Eurail Pass, P.O. Box 325, Old Greenwich, CT 06870.

To inquire about or purchase Eurail Passes, Britrail Passes, or Studentrail Passes, call Foremost Eurocar at 800-423-3111 (800-272-3299 in California), or write to Eurail Passes by Experts on Budget Travel, 35 W. 8th St., New York, NY 10011, 212-254-7474. **Note: you must purchase your pass before leaving the United States.**

Other Public Transportation

Public transportation is excellent all over Europe. Obtain a map and figure out where you want to go before you get on the streetcar, subway, or bus. Be sure you know where to purchase a ticket. Recently, in Italy, all twenty-one members of an American tour group were arrested for riding the bus without tickets. They hadn't realized that bus tickets could not be purchased on board the bus. Eurail and other discount passes are often valid on other public transportation, and information will be included with the pass you purchase.

Taxis

Although American taxi drivers have gained notoriety for taking you *anywhere* the long way around, their counterparts in Europe will usually give you rides that are direct and reasonably priced.

While the availability of cheap public transportation in the form of buses, trams, and subways normally makes a taxi the number-two choice of thrifty travelers overseas, at certain times it is a godsend. If you are driving yourself and get lost, call a taxi to lead you to your destination. You must pay the taxi fare, but it's simpler than asking directions for the twentieth time—and surer, too, since many people will give you directions even when they don't understand where it is you want to go.

. . . Two If by Sea

Ocean voyages, once the only way to travel from one continent to another, have gained a great deal in popularity in the last 20 to 30 years. Today's ships offer the traveler a way to get away from it all, without leaving the luxuries of life behind.

Cruises

An increasing number of vacationers are succumbing to the romantic lure of being pampered aboard a cruise ship. As airfare becomes more expensive, the cost of a cruise becomes more attractive. Travelers fed up with juggling admission fees, taxes, meal tabs, and prime hotel rates can discover the sweet sensation of top-drawer travel with a single price tag.

The point of taking a cruise is the trip itself. Select your destination from a variety of exotic locales and enjoy yourself all the way there, with dining, nightclubbing, and outdoor games.

Find out what isn't covered before you buy your ticket.

There are a couple of things to remember about cruises. First, you pay for the level of comfort in your stateroom. A less expensive one is likely to be small, below decks, and without a porthole. Second, while one of the benefits of a cruise is that all food, entertainment, and lodging are covered in the price of your ticket, you should find out what *isn't* covered before you buy your ticket. Possible extras include airfare to and from the starting point of the cruise and land tours at ports of call.

Freighters

Imagine a night of swirling fog, with Humphrey Bogart leaning over the ship's railing looking moodily out to sea . . . Although such an image is 1940ish, today's freighter offers up-to-date cruising without the crowds and false gaiety of planned recreation.

Freighters are large and carry heavy cargo, so they ride low in the water, providing a smoother ride than most cruise ships. And they're inexpensive, averaging half the price for comparable quarters on a cruise liner.

Because a freighter's principal occupation is carrying cargo, you won't be traveling on a rigid time schedule. Be prepared for delays and changes of itinerary. The number of days or hours the ship spends in port—and even whether the ship stops in a given port—depends on its cargo. You are free to watch the crew at work, loaf in your cabin with a good book, or wander into town to see the sights when in port.

If you'd like to cruise with an intimate company of eight to twelve fellow passengers, stay in modest-but-comfortable quarters and have lots of time to relax, then freighter travel is for you. There's usually a waiting list for freighter accommodations in the summer, so pick up some freighter schedules and make your reservations early. *Ford's Freighter Travel Guide,* updated annually by Ford's Travel Guides, 19448 Londilius Street, Northridge, CA 91324, provides year-round schedules of passenger-carrying freighters and a directory of travel agents specializing in freighter travel.

Cruise with an intimate company of eight to twelve fellow passengers.

Ferries

Looking for something in between the spartan comforts of a freighter and the constant entertainment of a cruise ship? Ferries are modern, spacious ships offering good food, comfortable cabins, and fabulous views. The taxis of the seagoing world, ferries offer economical transportation from one port to another. Large, utilitarian, yet exciting, ferries plow their way along the seacoasts and across the narrow channels separating the great cities of the world.

Going to Oslo from Copenhagen or from Paris to London? Planning to go to British Columbia from Seattle? Trains and buses, as well as private cars, are loaded into the bellies of the big boats for the journey, which can take as long as eighteen hours. You don't have to take a car onto the ferry. On most large ferries you can choose the accommodations that suit you: passage only (but be aware that no seat is guaranteed); reclining seat; dormitory with nonprivate bunks; two-, three-, or four-berth interior or exterior cabins, with or without lavatories; or first class with full bathing and lavatory facilities. Most cabins are clean and utilitarian; some are on a par with ocean-liner staterooms. Good food and some entertainment are available on a pay-as-you-go basis.

Ferries are ideal for the independent traveler, because they offer port-to-port travel and provide access to a whole coastline without the need for a car. You can get off at any stop you choose, catching the next ferry when you're ready to move on again. A

A ferryliner trip costs a fraction of the price of a regular cruise.

ferryliner trip costs a fraction of the price of a regular cruise—usually under $100 a day, compared to over $200 a day on a cruise.

Ferryliner Vacations in North America, by Michael and Laura Murphy (published by E. P. Dutton), and *Traveler's Guide to the Ocean Ferryliners of Europe,* volumes 1 and 2, by the same authors (published by Hippocrene Books, Inc.) will provide you with schedules, prices, and descriptions of most of the ferryliners operating today.

Barges

Imagine floating down an inland waterway on a flat-bottomed boat that doubles as a hotel. Long, starlit nights are interrupted only by the swish of the river and the plop of a fish rising to a june bug; on bright, sunshiny days, passing villages are reflected on the surface of the water.

These floating accommodations range from modest houseboats to luxury hotels, at prices that vary according to your requirements. Renting a houseboat for a family of four for a week will cost about the same as renting a summer cottage, and a cabin on a luxury barge is about the same price as a room in a quality hotel.

Glide along country canals.

One barge company, Waterways of France, offers an unforgettable experience aboard a luxury hotel barge. Gliding along country canals past vineyards and farms, dining on fine French cuisine aboard ship, you will be able to see life in France untrammeled by souvenir stands and tour buses. If a barge was good enough for Cleopatra, it ought to be worth a try! For more information, contact French Country Waterways, LTD, P.O. Box 2195, Duxbury, MA 02331, 800-222-1236.

ALONE OR WITH A GROUP?

Some like the security of the herd, while others like to lone-wolf it. Here's a mini-quiz to help you decide whether you should travel with a group or go solo. Select the response that's most like what you would do.

1. You've been invited to a cocktail party where the

only person you know is the host. You . . .

a. stick close to the host so he or she can introduce you

b. introduce yourself to most of the other guests

c. spend most of your time at the snack table

2. You've been waiting some time at a jewelry counter for a salesclerk to help you. When it's finally your turn, she waits on someone else. You . . .

a. tell the manager

b. say "Pardon me, but I was next"

c. say nothing

3. You're stranded for forty-eight hours in a strange city. You . . .

a. call a friend

b. pick up a travel guide and see the sights

c. swim in the hotel pool and watch TV

4. You're flying to London today. You arrive at the airport . . .

Test your travel taste.

a. before the other passengers

b. about the same time as everybody else

c. just as the last passengers are boarding

5. When you travel, your luggage is usually . . .

a. two or three pieces of a matched set

b. limited to what you can carry

c. several paper bags

6. When you travel, you set the highest priority on . . .

a. seeing all the sights

b. having a good time

c. taking pictures of the places you've been

7. When it comes to reading a map, you would . . .

a. prefer to let somebody else do it

b. have little or no problem reaching your destination

c. probably never find your way to your destination

8. Your last vacation was . . .

a. a tour or cruise arranged through a travel agent

b. planned by reading travel books or asking friends

c. spur-of-the-moment

9. You spend most of your travel dollars on . . .

a. accommodations, transportation, and admission

b. transportation

c. accommodations, transportation, and souvenirs

10. In college classrooms, you usually sat . . .

a. in the middle of the room

b. in the front of the room

c. in the back of the room

If most of your answers are "a," you are a punctual, precise person who prefers to let others take care of you. Travel with a group would be ideal for you if you can accept others' imperfections.

If most of your answers are "b," you are a self-starter and enjoy making your own plans. You'd do better alone.

If most of your answers are "c," you need a little help getting organized. You might drive the "a" traveler crazy if you wound up on the same tour, but traveling with a group will ensure that you get to see and do all the things you dream about.

Finding a Suitable Traveling Companion

Most tours and cruises are planned with couples in mind. You'll pay 30 to 50 percent more for a single room, so from a financial standpoint it's worth it to have a roommate.

You'll pay 30 to 50 percent more to travel alone.

How can you find one? Your travel agent or tour director will usually try to match up other singles, if asked. Another possibility is an agency that introduces single travelers who are in search of agreeable partners. One such agency is Travel Companion Exchange; contact them at Box 833, Amityville, NY 11071, 516-454-0080, for membership information.

ACCOMMODATIONS

Wherever you stay, at the Hilton or in a friend's spare bedroom, it's wise to remember basic security rules.

If you are staying in a quality hotel, you can deposit your valuables in the hotel safe. Most airports and train stations have pay lockers where you can leave extra baggage in relative safety. Otherwise, keep your valuables with you—*not* on the dresser or in your luggage. Better yet, don't take expensive jewelry, radios, or watches at all.

Never leave your passport or money unattended. In some countries you will be required to turn your passport in to the hotel for registration. While it's secure there, you should reclaim it if at all possible. One reason is that you may need your passport in order to cash traveler's checks. Another is that if you get into any trouble, the first thing the authorities will ask for is your passport.

Never leave your passport or money unattended.

If you're staying in dormitories or hostels, try to choose one with a night attendant or a curfew. There will be less crime when the entrances are controlled.

Appendix 2, at the end of this book, contains addresses and telephone numbers for government-run tourist offices operating within the United States. Many states and foreign countries provide free or inexpensive pamphlets on request that list accommodations. It's worth a telephone call or letter to find out what's available.

Hotels

Although the American penchant for rating things— movies and restaurants, for example—has not yet produced a nationwide system for evaluating hotels, in other countries the situation is different. Around the world, hotels are rated by a star system—four stars for top-of-the-line luxury, three stars for quality, two stars for spartan comfort, and one star for economy.

While even the cheapest American motel provides individual showers and toilets, not every hotel overseas boasts these amenities. For those who are willing to share a bathroom or to walk down the hall to a toilet, economy hotels can be a bargain if they offer a good location and clean sheets.

Small Hotels and Inns

Small hotels are often more secure than big hotels, since the little places shut down at night. If you go out, you have to request a key or ring the night bell for admittance.

In France, a small hotel is called a *pension;* in Germany, it's a *Gasthaus.* At these and similar small hotels in other countries, you'll usually get clean lodgings (with shared bathrooms) and a continental breakfast at a reasonable rate. (Beware, however, of pensions and guest houses that require you to purchase half or full board with your room—they're usually expensive.)

The best guide to this sort of accommodation is the *Michelin Red Guide* series, which lists all the places to stay in the countries it covers.

Bed-and-Breakfasts

Bed and breakfast in Britain.

In North America and Great Britain, bed-and-breakfasts fill the same niche as the small hotels in other countries. B & Bs, as they're called, are quite different in the U.S. than elsewhere. Here, they're usually tony little hotels and not always inexpensive. In Great Britain, where they originated, B & Bs are often genteel homes opened to a few visitors.

Generally, you get a hearty breakfast, friendly conversation, and a shared bathroom along with your lodgings. The best guides to what's available are *The Complete Guide to Bed & Breakfasts, Inns, & Guest-*

houses, by Pamela Lanier (published by John Muir Publications), and *Fodor's Bed & Breakfast Guide,* by Mary Winget (published by Fodor's Travel Publications, Inc.).

An American bed-and-breakfast with a fellow educator as your host or hostess might be just your cup of tea. Write to La Verne Long, 317 Piedmont Rd., Santa Barbara, CA 93105 for a list of teachers who provide B & B accommodations for other teachers.

Country Inns

Country inns are another possibility. In France, such an accommodation is called a *gite* (pronounced "zheet"). You and your family can rent a cottage house, part of an inn, or an entire floor of a vacation home in the French countryside, by the month or week, for an average weekly cost of $140 for a family of five. Contact Maison Du Tourisme Vert, Gites de France, 35, Rue Godot-de-Mauroy, 75000 Paris, France; or Agriculture et Tourisme, 9, Avenue Gerges V, 75008, Paris, France.

Rent a French country house.

The Japanese city of Gifu, a craft center two hours west of Tokyo, offers free lodging and meals supplied by 400 hosts. Guests may stay up to seven nights. (Applications are taken on a first-come, first-served basis.) Contact Yoshinori Toyoda, Gifu Prefecture, c/o Juroku Bank Ltd., One World Trade Center, Suite 8353, New York, NY 10048. If you miss out on the free accommodations, you can still save money in Japan by skipping the Western-style hotels and staying at traditional inns called *ryokans.* The Japanese National Tourist Organization will send you a pamphlet (see Appendix 2).

Lodge for free in Japan.

In Germany, families often take a whole month for a restful vacation at a farm or remote cabin. You can do the same thing. Horseback riding, wine-tasting tours, and hunting and fishing trips are available. Contact the German National Tourist Office (see Appendix 2).

Similar programs are available through the Irish Tourist Board, British Tourist Authority, New Zealand Travel Hosts (Attention: June Hawes, 279 Williams St., Kaiapoi, Canterbury, New Zealand),

Spanish National Tourist Office, Australian Hostels Travel Network (2500 Wilshire Blvd., Suite 507, Los Angeles, CA 90057, 213-380-2184), and the Swiss National Tourist Office.

Farm, Ranch & Country Vacations by Pat Dickerman (published by Farm & Ranch Publications) is a complete guide to vacations in the rural United States. You can help out on a working ranch, relax and be taken care of, camp in your motor home, or vacation with your own horse, depending on the farm or ranch you select. It includes a special section on places for teens.

Other Options

You have many alternatives to staying at expensive hotel chains, options that will spare your pocketbook and give you a chance to really experience life in the place you are visiting. Following are a few of the best.

College Dorms

You can save more than 50 percent over conventional lodging by staying at a college or university, and eating meals at the campus cafeteria means additional savings.

College dorms are clean, safe, and comfortable—but don't expect anyone to carry your luggage or park your car! Rooms usually feature twin beds and a variety of bathroom options (shared bath, attached bath between two rooms, or private bath). Desks and chairs are provided in each room, and there is usually a television in a shared lounge area. Air conditioning and linen are usually available.

You should bring linen and towels (just in case), sleeping bags for children (who may be able to sleep free in your room), cookware and utensils if you intend to stay a while (many colleges offer limited cooking facilities), golf clubs, tennis rackets, swimsuits, and cameras.

Book college rooms in advance. Book university accommodations in advance, specifying the dates you wish to stay and the number in your party. (Note that because many universities host conferences, you may need to be flexible about dates.) Include a deposit, and reconfirm the prices and types of accommodations available. If you have any questions, ask about restrictions and rules (such as the policy on pets and whether you can get a refund if your plans change) before you send any money.

The *U.S. and Worldwide Travel Accommodations Guide* is the only comprehensive source of information about the availability of dorms to travelers. It lists more than 650 universities and colleges here and abroad that welcome guests; in addition, it lists other inexpensive accommodations and provides dozens of helpful hints for travelers. To order, send $11.95 to Campus Travel Service, P.O. Box 5007, Laguna Beach, CA 92652.

If France is your destination, you can obtain a free university pass that provides dormitory lodging for about eight dollars a night. Five thousand rooms are available for summer stays in such cities as Bayonne and Fontainebleau. Contact the International Friendship Service, Attn.: Penny Walsh, 22994 El Toro Road, El Toro, CA 92630, 714-458-8868.

Five thousand rooms in France.

YMCAs

Inexpensive lodging can be obtained at YMCA residences open to the general public. The *U.S. and Worldwide Travel Accommodations Guide* lists YMCA lodging centers in the U.S., Canada, and overseas. The cost of a room is usually $12–$25 a night.

The YMCA provides single and double rooms for both men and women. Children are welcome if accompanied by an adult. Fitness facilities are available, as well as tourist information. Reserve rooms directly by calling the YMCA lodging center you wish to stay at, or book reservations through The Y's Way, 356 W. 34th St., New York, NY 10001, 212-760-5856/-5857/-5892/-5840. Reservations must be paid in advance by traveler's check, U.S. money order, or certified check. Visa and MasterCard are accepted if the booking is arranged two months before the date of arrival. NO personal checks, postal or telegraph payments, or money orders are accepted.

Children are welcome at the YMCA.

(YWCAs usually offer lodging for women only, and guests are required to join the association. Write to YWCA, 726 Broadway, New York, NY 10003, 212-614-2700.)

Youth Hostels

Youth hostels, for years the choice of young people seeing the world cheaply, offer low-cost lodging for all ages. Preference is given to those under thirty, but there's usually room for older travelers, as long as they're willing to stay in a dormitory and change their own sheets.

Members of American Youth Hostels (AYH) receive a hosteling membership card that is honored worldwide for admission to International Youth Hostel Federation (IYHF) hostels. There are 270 hostels in the U.S., where you'll pay roughly $6–$13 per night. Send $3 to American Youth Hostels, P.O. Box 37613, Dept. 950, Washington, D.C. 20013, 202-783-6161 for a booklet containing descriptions of every American hostel (including maps and directions). On the West Coast, contact AYH, Los Angeles Council, 335 W. 7th St., San Pedro, CA 90731, 213-831-8848.

Hostels in Israel.

Youth and Student Adventures lists thirty-one youth hostels and thirty-eight Christian hospices that offer budget accommodations for visitors to Israel. Contact the Israel Government Tourist Office, 6380 Wilshire Blvd., Suite 1700, Los Angeles, CA 90048, 213-568-7462.

You can visit sunny California and stay for only $10 a night (children traveling with their parents stay for half price) at the California Hostel Experience. Thirty-one hostels scattered across the state are waiting for you. Contact American Youth Hostels, 425 Divisadero, Suite 307, San Francisco, CA 94117, 415-863-9939.

Renting a Home Overseas

Exchange homes for a brief stay.

Families or groups might be interested in renting a home abroad. At Home Abroad, Sutton Town House, 405 E. 56th St., 6H, New York, NY 10022 offers hundreds of homes in all price categories for your holiday. If an apartment or home in London is your heart's desire, write to London Homes, P.O. Box 730, London, SW6 2QN, England (the minimum stay is two weeks).

Trading Places

Educators around the world want to trade places with you, wherever you live. Three programs exclusively for teachers enable them—and you—to find homes to stay in for a short time. Teacher Swap, Box 4130, Rocky Point, NY 11778 sells a directory that lists homes in thirty-seven states and in Canada, West Germany, Austria, England, and the Virgin Islands.

A similar program sponsored by the American Federation of Teachers and Britain's National Association of Schoolmasters/University Women Teachers puts you in touch with families wanting to trade homes and automobiles for a minimum of a week's stay. The enrollment fee is $25. Obtain an application from AFT Travel, 555 New Jersey Ave., N.W., Washington, D.C. 20001, 201-879-4424.

A third vacation-home exchange exclusively for educators promises to save you 50 to 80 percent of the cost of a vacation in the U.S., Canada, or Great Britain. Write to Teachers Travel Unlimited, P.O. Box 900, Morrisburg, Ontario, Canada.

Taking Care of Business

I f there's one thing teachers know a lot about, it's paperwork. Grading projects, essays, reports, and homework; filling out report cards and evaluations; and collecting assignments and notes from home occupy a major part of an educator's time—and rightly so, because it's important to collect and share information about our students.

There's a lot of paperwork involved with travel.

There's a lot of paperwork involved with travel, too, even travel within the United States. Itineraries must be made and distributed to those who need them, maps collected, hotel reservations applied for (and confirmations kept in a safe place), tickets purchased, and so forth. If you intend to go outside the country, you will have other applications to submit and documents to keep, all for the same purpose: to present organized information about yourself to the authorities, whether they be hotel desk clerks or ambassadors.

Start the wheels in motion on this paperwork as

early as possible. An otherwise well-planned vacation can be ruined because of a passport that never turns up or a visa that can't be obtained at the last minute. Once you have received your precious pieces of paper or official stamps, keep them safe in a special folder or briefcase until you set off on your journey.

IMPORTANT DOCUMENTS

Passports

Your passport, issued by the Department of State, Washington, D.C., allows you to leave and return to the country. It identifies you as a U.S. citizen and is valid for ten years.

Passport applications can be found at the U.S. Government Passport Services Offices and at some post offices and county court clerks' offices. You will have to apply in person. (If you have obtained a passport previously, you can file an application for a new passport by mail.) If you have never applied for a passport before, you will need to submit the following:

• a birth certificate (NOT a reproduction—it must have a registrar's signature and seal) or certificate of naturalization

• two identical photographs, taken not more than six months ago

• identification, such as a driver's license, with your signature and photograph or physical description on it

At the time of this publication, a passport costs $42 plus a $7 execution fee. With parental permission, persons under eighteen can obtain a five-year passport for $27.

The busiest time in the passport office is between March and August, so apply in plenty of time for all your paperwork to be processed—several months before you are due to leave. Allow a week or two extra if you also need a visa.

The busiest time in the passport office is between March and August.

When traveling, keep your passport with you. You can purchase a pouch that will hang around your neck or go around your waist like a belt. (Council Travel offices, subsidiaries of the Council on International Educational Exchange, carry these indispensable items for travelers. Call the CIEE's New York office at 212-661-1450 for the location of one near you.) Put your traveler's checks, passport, and part of your money in the pouch, and wear it inside your clothing.

Photocopy your passport.

If your passport is lost or stolen, report the loss immediately to local police and to Passport Services, Department of State, Washington, D.C. 20520, 202-647-0581. If you are overseas, contact the nearest U.S. consulate or embassy. Replacing your passport can take a couple of weeks if the consulate has to start from scratch. A photocopy of your passport, a certified birth certificate, and two passport photos tucked in your suitcase at the beginning of your trip can cut the waiting time for a replacement passport down to a few days.

Visas/Tourist Cards

In addition to passports, some foreign countries require that you apply for official permission—a visa—to visit them. A visa is a stamp put in your passport by a foreign country allowing you to visit there for a limited length of time. There are different types of visas, such as student visas and tourist visas, each with its own time limit.

Usually, you must obtain a visa before leaving the United States. Ask your travel agent to help you get a visa, or apply directly to the embassy or consulate of the country you plan to visit. Expect to pay a small fee for a visa. The process can take a week or two, so apply well in advance of your departure date. For complete information on visa requirements, send a stamped, self-addressed, business-size envelope to the Bureau of Consular Affairs, CA/PA Room 2807, Department of State, Washington, D.C. 20520, and ask for the booklet *Visa Requirements of Foreign Countries.*

Countries that have close ties with the United

States, such as Mexico and Canada, do not require visiting Americans to obtain either a passport or a visa. If your stay will be less than twenty-four hours, you can enter by simply showing your driver's license. For longer stays, you must have a tourist card, which you will be required to fill out prior to crossing the border. There may be a small fee for the card.

Certificate of Vaccination

Some foreign countries may require you to be immunized against yellow fever, cholera, or other diseases. You will have to show proof that you have had the required vaccinations before you can enter the country. International vaccination requirements change often. Check with the U.S. Public Health Service, your state health department, or the consulate of the country you wish to visit.

When you plan your trip, arrange an appointment with your doctor at least eight weeks prior to your departure to get your immunizations up to date. Your doctor will provide you with a yellow, passport-size record of the date of vaccination and the types of vaccines used. Obtain prescriptions for any medications you normally take, and ask the doctor's advice about what to put in your traveling first-aid kit.

See your doctor well in advance.

Documentation for Drivers

Most countries will allow you to drive using your state driver's license as long as you hold a valid passport, but some require that you carry a translation of your license. The International Driver's Permit solves this problem (it's written in nine languages) and is accepted in most countries. The permit can be obtained from any American Automobile Association office for about $5.

If you intend to take your own car with you overseas, you will need a national mark plate (an oval decal reading "U.S.A.") to place on the rear of your car, as well as a *green card*—an international motor insurance card obtainable from your automobile insurance company.

Although it's expensive, renting a car overseas is

Auto insurance overseas.

easier than ferrying one with you (see chapter 2 for some agencies in the States that rent cars for use overseas). You will need an international driver's permit and a credit card to rent a car. If your insurance will cover you while you're driving overseas, bring documentation of that coverage. Some credit cards automatically provide auto insurance for rental cars when you charge the rental fees. Otherwise, you will have to purchase insurance from the car-rental agency.

International Student or Teacher I.D. Cards

Those who traveled extensively as students will remember the International Student I.D. Card (ISIC) with fondness. Students over twelve years of age enrolled in an educational program leading to a degree can purchase this internationally recognized card and receive discounts on transportation, accommodations, and entry to museums, theaters, cultural events, and historical sites.

Discounts for educators.

An International Teacher I.D. Card is now available, which aims to offer the same discounts to educators. Teachers can save up to 40 percent on flights between the U.S. and Latin America, Australia, or Asia, and other destinations may be added as the program is developed. Other benefits include automatic medical coverage until the expiration of the card, and a 10 percent discount on Eurocentre Teaching Refresher Courses.

Both cards can be purchased through Council Travel Services, a division of CIEE with more than thirty offices worldwide. Contact CIEE at 212-661-1450 for the office nearest you.

TRAVEL INSURANCE

Nobody likes to think about the possibility of an interrupted vacation, but such things do happen. Recently the television news featured the plight of a group of high-school students left waiting at the airport for tickets that never arrived because the company that was supposed to have arranged their travel had gone bankrupt. Could that happen to you?

Taking Care of Business

Travel insurance saves you worry and, in the event that something does go wrong, provides assistance when you need it most. Many travel agents offer this type of insurance, and it's also available through some local teachers associations (ask about Access America, a subsidiary of Blue Cross and Blue Shield). Assist-A-Card, an emergency service, charges a flat fee that's scaled according to how long you'll be gone and promises personal emergency services. For information on their coverage, contact Assist-A-Card Corporation of America, 347 Fifth Avenue, New York, NY 10016. Some credit cards automatically grant limited insurance when you charge a trip.

Following are descriptions of some different types of travel insurance that may be part of a package offered through your travel agent, credit card company, or teachers' union:

Trip-Cancellation Insurance

Suppose you become ill the day before the trip and have to cancel out. Or some catastrophe at home forces you to cut short your three-week cruise. Or suppose the airline you've bought tickets from cancels your flight, goes on strike, or even goes out of business.

Trip-cancellation insurance can protect your payment or nonrefundable deposit when a trip must be cancelled due to serious injury, illness, or death (whether yours or that of a family member or traveling companion), or other unforeseen circumstances, such as the default of an airline, tour operator, or cruise line. If you expect to spend $1,000 or more on your tour, cruise, or other type of travel, trip-cancellation insurance is strongly recommended.

If you didn't buy tour insurance and you have to cancel your trip, there's a ray of hope. Although most package trips, cruises, and low-cost airfare schemes contain clauses that limit or deny refunds if you are unable to use your ticket, in some instances you may be able to recover all or part of your investment.

If you are unable to take or continue your planned vacation because of one of the reasons usually covered by trip-cancellation insurance, write a

What if you don't have insurance?

letter to the tour operator documenting your situation, and send one copy to your travel agent. It may take some time, but if your reasons for cancellation are compelling enough, you ought to get a refund.

Baggage Insurance/Baggage and Travel Delay Insurance

Less earth-shattering, but still enough to ruin a vacation, are lost luggage and unforeseen delays. Where will you get immediate cash to rent a room or replace those essential items that went to Valhalla with your luggage? This type of insurance pays for loss or damage to your luggage and personal effects as well as the cost of additional accommodations or travel expenses when you are delayed by lost luggage or airline cancellations.

Health or Medical Insurance

Check the fine print in your policy.

Most people don't know that standard health insurance usually doesn't cover medical care or hospitalization abroad. Check the fine print in your policy. Will it pay for medical care if you fall in Bombay and require hospitalization? Will you be reimbursed for X rays in Naples? If not, you should obtain specialized health insurance for the duration of your trip.

Features to look for in traveler's health insurance:

1. *Medical Expenses.* Pays on-the-spot medical bills, including hospital charges.

2. *Travel Accidents.* Pays if you are killed or disabled while aboard an airliner.

3. *Medical Transportation.* Pays for transportation to an adequate facility or return to the U.S. for hospitalization, if necessary, including transportation for a medical escort and next of kin.

Traveler's Medical Insurance

While most traveler's insurance includes both trip-cancellation and health insurance, it is possible to obtain traveler's medical insurance by itself.

If you purchase your traveler's checks from Bank of America, you can buy a forty-five-day travel medical-insurance policy for only $8.50. Ask your travel agent or local Bank of America branch about the Bank America Safe Travel Network, or call 415-624-1623.

Save through teachers' organizations.

A one-year policy available from Travel Assistance International provides up to $5,000 in medical costs and unlimited transportation for medical assistance. Contact TIA at 1133 15th St. NW, Suite 400, Washington, D.C., 800-821-2828.

MAIL

There are two ways to get mail or messages while traveling in Europe without a set itinerary.

American Express

American Express offices in Europe will hold letters for owners of American Express traveler's checks, although not all will accept bulky parcels. Mail is returned if not claimed within thirty days. Ask your local American Express office for the booklet listing full-service offices.

European Post Offices

Mail addressed to you in care of *Poste Restante* ("Hold for Delivery") at a European post office will be held for you, although you may have to pay a small fee when you pick it up.

Because American handwriting can be difficult for people of other nationalities to read, have correspondents print your name as it appears on your passport and underline your last name. If a letter does get lost in transit, ask the postal clerk to look under your first name. It wouldn't be a bad idea, either, to check at the city's main post office and at the one nearest the railroad station.

MONEY-SAVING PROGRAMS AND OFFERS

There's no denying that on a teacher's salary it makes sense to stretch a dollar bill until George Washington says "Ouch!" There are many special programs that you can take advantage of—some of them available through your state association or national teachers' union—that offer great savings on fares, tours, accommodations, car rentals, and things to do once you've reached your destination.

Because the price and exact details of such programs change often, the information here is intended as a general guideline only. For exact and current information, consult the offering agency.

Teachers' Unions and Associations

Who knows teachers better than other teachers?

Who knows teachers better than other teachers? Your national union and local association have many travel programs tailored to suit your needs. They're usually the first place you should look for a tour or cruise, because they work for you and can obtain savings through quantity buying. These services can save you time and money, whether you select one of their packaged tours or take advantage of the discount rates you can obtain on rooms and car rentals.

National Education Association

The NEA travel program has been sponsoring vacations for members for more than forty years (contact NEA Travel, 800-637-4636). NEA's popular vacations take members to Europe, Russia, China, the South Pacific, Africa, and the Americas. NEA members also receive discounts of 5–15 percent on car rentals through the Hertz Corporation.

NEA programs are not limited to overseas travel.

NEA programs are not limited to overseas travel, however. Members are also offered a 5 percent discount on all American Express vacations in the U.S. and Canada. For those who like to go it alone, extensive land-only, land-and-air, and air-only packages are available.

If your dream is to find excitement and adventure, you can book an Adventure Tour, run by the renowned Sobek Expeditions. Raft down the Colorado, explore the Amazon, or hike the Galapagos Islands.

For an educational summer, attend NEA's symposium at Britain's historic Oxford University. (For more information on this program, see chapter 6.)

Other kinds of programs include the all-inclusive Jack Tar resorts, located in five different areas of the Caribbean and Mexico. The set price includes accommodations, all meals, unlimited drinks, and activities.

Benefits available to all NEA members and their travel companions include these:

1. An escrow account that insures the return of your deposit if the trip is cancelled.

2. Guaranteed prices.

3. Deposit of only $50 for most programs.

4. No cancellation fee for cancellation up to sixty days before departure.

5. Free American Express traveler's checks.

6. Comprehensive travel insurance at reasonable rates.

7. Group travel discounts.

8. NEA-Retired discounts.

American Federation of Teachers

Members of the American Federation of Teachers can obtain hefty discounts by using AFT Travel. Be prepared to show your union card when asking for your discount.

AFT TRAVEL BENEFITS

International/Domestic Travel Packages

1. *AFT Tour Packages or "Flights-Only."* Choose from budget, first-class, or deluxe tour packages to Europe, the U.S., Canada, the Caribbean, Africa, the South Pacific, and the Orient. Trips and

"flights-only" are featured regularly in the AFT magazine *American Teacher,* or write to AFT Travel for descriptive brochures. Programs are available year-round.

2. *AFT Discount-Travel Card.* Book short-notice vacation packages over the twenty-four-hour hot line, and still get up to 60 percent off the regular price, a 5 percent cash bonus on scheduled airfare, and a 7 percent cash bonus on most cruises, charters, and tour packages. The discount does *not* include regular, ongoing programs. Family memberships cost $19.95 per year.

3. *Home-Exchange Program.* See chapter 2 for details of this program, which offers home exchange with British teachers. The one-time application fee is $25.

Hotel Discounts

1. *AFT Hotel-Discount Plan.* Obtain exclusive AFT rates (based on hotel availability) of up to 50 percent off regular room rates at hotels in Washington, D.C., Boston, New York City, Detroit, New Orleans, Chicago, Orlando, San Francisco, Los Angeles, and Tampa. Make reservations through AFT Travel in writing at least two weeks prior to arrival date.

2. *Nationwide Hotel Discounts.* Over 450 Travelodge motor hotels throughout North America and more than 150 Rodeway Inns coast-to-coast offer a 10 percent discount on regular rates to AFT members. Call Travelodge Central Reservations at 800-255-3050 or Rodeway Inns Central Reservations at 800-228-2000 and identify yourself as an AFT member.

3. *Raddison Hotel executive program.* Receive a 5 percent discount on Raddison's already discounted corporate single rates (a companion stays free in the same room) at more than 100 Raddison hotels located in 34 states, Canada, Mexico, and the Dominican Republic. Benefits include the best room available at the time of check-in, a free newspaper each morning, and Frequent Guest Awards. For

reservations and information, call 800-333-3333 and identify yourself as a member of the AFT/ R.E.P. Program #1260.

4. *Holiday Inns.* More than 25 Holiday Inns in cities such as Philadelphia, New Orleans, Dallas, Los Angeles, Chicago, and Seattle offer 10 to 25 percent off their regular rates to union members. More information is available from AFT Travel.

Car-Rental Discounts

1. *National Car Rental.* Members receive a 20 percent discount on National's business rate when renting a car of any size, and a 10 percent discount on many special rates, including weekend specials, weekly rates (except prepaids), monthly specials, promotional specials, and one-way rentals. Also included are discounts of 10—15 percent on overseas rentals. This program requires a special I.D. card, available from AFT Travel or your union representative.

2. *Alamo Rent-A-Car.* Alamo, with 65 locations nationwide, including Hawaii, offers union members special rates that range from $28 per day for an economy car to $34 for a full-sized car, and comparable savings on weekly rates. All rates include unlimited mileage. This program also requires a special I.D. card, available from AFT Travel or your union representative.

Theme-Park Discounts

The following theme parks offer free membership cards that entitle you to discounts on admission, restaurants, and lodging:

1. *Walt Disney Magic Kingdom Club.* Disney World, EPCOT Center, MGM studio tour theme park, and Disneyland.

2. *Wild World Card.* Wild World amusement park, located near Washington, D.C. Open summers only.

3. *"Passport Club" to Busch Gardens.* Busch Gardens in Williamsburg, Virginia (open summers only), and Adventure Island in Tampa, Fla.

4. *Marine World/Africa USA Wild Card.* Africa USA theme park, located near San Francisco.

5. *Universal Studios Fan-Club Card.* Studios and theme park, located in Los Angeles/Hollywood.

6. *Sea World Club Card.* Sea World in San Diego, Calif.; Orlando, Fla.; Aurora, Ohio; and San Antonio, Tex. Also Cypress Gardens in Central Florida and Boardwalk and Baseball near Orlando, Fla.

7. *Action Park/Vernon Valley/Great Gorge Club Card.* Year-round resort located one hour from New York in Vernon, N.J. Discounts on skiing, lift tickets, activities, and accommodations.

8. *Sesame Place Fun-Club Card.* Children's theme park near Langhorne, Pa.

For more information, call 202-879-4424, or write to the American Federation of Teachers, AFL-CIO, 555 New Jersey Avenue, NW, Washington, D.C. 20001, Attn.: Travel.

Local Associations

Several state teachers' associations affiliated with NEA offer their members travel programs that range from discounts on airfares, hotels/motels, and amusement parks to escorted tours and travel packages. While most states offer some travel benefits, California, Washington, Michigan, Wisconsin, Tennessee, Texas, and New Jersey lead the pack.

These programs pour forth a steady stream of discount tickets to ball games, amusement parks, and tours throughout the year. You can take trips to Disney World and EPCOT Center, to the Canadian Rockies or Washington, D.C., to the northeastern states to see the fall foliage, or to the cities of the deep South to take their spring home tours.

That's not all. In addition to cruises and tours at phenomenally low prices (for example, a savings of up to $832 per couple on a recent Caribbean Christmas tour offered through the California Teachers' Association) members-only travel clubs offer such bargains as half-price lodgings, notification of last-minute discount-travel opportunities, and a complete set of discount cards for regional entertainment attractions—all for a low membership fee of around $5. Ask your union headquarters or local union representative what services are available and how to get your name on the mailing list.

Inquire, too, about an Entertainment membership card. Through this, the world's largest discount club, you can obtain savings of up to 50 percent at hotels and restaurants, plus big savings on cruises, tours, resort condo vacations, and auto rentals.

BARGAIN AIRFARE

Charters

The cheapest way to fly is by charter, although special promotions and buy-ahead tickets give the charter companies a run for their money. For information on charter flights to Europe, contact: Continental Travel Shop, 213-393-2093; Dollar-stretchers, 800-669-9985; DER Tours, 213-394-0288; Jet Vacations, 213-652-0999. Destinations include Frankfurt, London, Paris, Amsterdam, and Düsseldorf.

Economy Travel Agents

Farefinders, 251 South Robertson, Beverly Hills, CA 90211, 213-652-6305, specializes in finding the cheapest flights for its clients. There's no fee for the service.

Ticket Brokers

If you have to fly somewhere at the last minute and don't want to pay full fees, try a ticket broker. Through a service such as UniTravel, you can get fares that are almost as good as charter fares, since ticket brokers purchase thousands of tickets in bulk. Options include staying abroad for as long as a year, or arriving at one destination and departing from another.

Flying at the last minute; save money anyway.

The reservation center is open Monday through Saturday, and tickets are delivered by Federal Express. Write for a brochure: UniTravel, P.O. Box 16220, St. Louis, MO 63150.

For airfares that put the smallest dent in your pocketbook, keep the following points in mind:

- Nonstop travel costs more than travel involving one or more stops.

- The lowest airfares to Europe are available between September 15 and May 14.

- Buying a round-trip fare in the U.S. is about 10 percent cheaper than buying two one-way tickets. (This does not hold true for tickets sold in Europe, however.)

- Special weekend-excursion rates—for example, between Los Angeles and New York—are nearly half the full fare. They must be bought in advance and are usually nonrefundable and nontransferable. You buy, you'd better fly.

- Night-coach fares are 20 percent cheaper than daytime fares.

Round-the-World Tickets

Round-the-World (RTW) tickets offer the best value for summer travel. For a price that's less than the cost of a round-trip ticket to any one country, you can visit six or seven. Your ticket is good for a whole year, and there's no minimum stay required at any point. You choose the time you fly. The European/Far East route flies to Honolulu, Taipei, Singapore, Athens, and Paris on Singapore Airlines, then to New York and Los Angeles on TWA. Alternate routes include New Zealand, Australia, Japan, Asia, Thailand, Hong Kong, India, Egypt, and Europe. Extra stops can be added for $25. The only catch to this bargain is that you can't reverse directions going around the globe.

Most international airlines offer RTW travel. Don't expect your travel agent to dig them up for you, though; the fare is so low that not much commission is paid. Instead, call 800-555-1212 for the airlines' toll-free numbers.

DISCOUNT TRAVEL

Travel Clubs

Discount-travel clubs can save you between 20 and 70 percent on regular cruise and tour fares, *if* you are willing to travel on short notice. This type of club is perfect for an exciting winter or spring break, or even for an unplanned summer getaway. Two that don't require membership fees are the Last-Minute Cruise Club, 870 9th St., San Pedro, CA 90731, 213-519-1717, and Spur-of-the-Moment Tours and Cruises, 1080 Jefferson Avenue, Culver City, CA 90230, 800-343-1991 (in California, call 213-839-2418); hot line, 213-838-9329. Both clubs send postcards listing the latest bargains.

Discount Coupons, Special Tickets, and Reduced Admission

Paying less than the full admission saves you money for other attractions. Ask your travel agent or inquire at state travel bureaus about discount coupons and two-for-one deals. Such offers change frequently, so it pays to check just before you leave. Here are a few that were current as this book went to press.

Paying less than the full admission saves you money for other attractions.

New York

Visiting the Big Apple? Write for a free, seventy-page directory of more than 200 hotel packages in New York City, some as inexpensive as $32 per person per night. Amenities include dining, museums, entertainment, free parking, and rooms with kitchenettes. NYC Visitors Bureau, c/o Packages, 2 Columbus Circle, New York, NY 10019.

Discount coupons for hotels, sightseeing attractions, museums, and restaurants in New York State and New York City offer two-for-one bargains. Call 800-225-5697 and ask for the "I Love New York Passport to Adventure" and the three other discount books.

Florida

Obtain similar discounts to attractions in Florida by sending $1 to Florida Travel Discount Guide, 618 S. Main St., Gainesville, FL 32601.

Yet another Florida discount book is free for the telephoning. Call 800-327-9159 and ask for the *Vacation Guide* and the *Getaway Coupon Book.* You will receive discount coupons to major attractions such as Busch Gardens, Spaceport USA, and Gatorland Zoo, as well as local restaurants.

The White House

There's no need to stand in long lines for a tour of the White House when you visit Washington, D.C. Contact your senator or representative for tickets to a free congressional tour of the public rooms of the White House. Requests should be made three months in advance. Send the dates you will be in the capital to your congressman in the Senate or your representative in the House of Representatives, Office Bldg., Washington, D.C. 20510.

Free Attractions

The world is filled with free places to visit and enjoy.

The world is filled with free places to visit and enjoy. Thousands of American parks, museums, factories, and zoos, and even the NASA space-launch site, can be visited at no cost. But don't stop your bargain hunting when you leave the U.S. borders. Several countries sell or give passes to tourists.

U.S.

Several books list free attractions inside the United States. The best of these include *Free Attractions, U.S.A.,* by Mary VanMeer and Michael Pasquarelli (published by East Woods Press); *The National Directory of Free Tourist Attractions* (published by Pilot Books); and the four-volume series *Best Free Attractions,* by John Whitman (published by Meadowbrook Press).

The Netherlands

Save 50 percent on trains in Holland.

The Holland Culture Card gives you entry to more than 200 art, historical, and special-interest museums in the Netherlands. It also chops a whopping 50 percent off first-class railway travel. For information, write to the Netherlands National Tourist Office (address at the back of this book).

Italy
The Italian State Museum Ticket provides free admission to many state-run museums, archaeological worlds of wonder, and art galleries across Italy. Purchase it from Alitalia Airlines, 666 Fifth Avenue, New York, NY 10019.

Ireland
The Irish Tourist Board will send you a list of eighty-one free attractions in the land of the Blarney Stone. Inquire at the Irish Tourist Board (address at the back of this book).

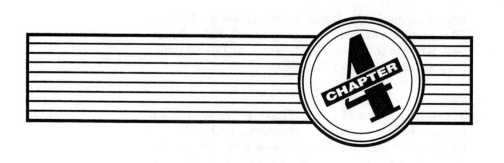

CHAPTER 4

Money Makes the World Go 'Round

Money can slip right through your fingers if it isn't handled with care—all the more reason to watch your centavos and pence when you're overseas. A little financial savvy will keep you from coming up short on your trip around the world.

FOREIGN CURRENCY

Change your money after you arrive.

Visitors from foreign countries are always a little amazed that you can't just walk into any bank in the United States and purchase marks or yen. Because our country is so large, most Americans have little need for that banking service, so it's handled by specialists.

Your personal bank *can* obtain foreign currency for you—but after a considerable wait and for a hefty fee. The vagaries of the dollar on the international currency market aside, you'll do best to purchase most of your foreign money *after* you reach your destination, at the exchanges or local banks. For one thing, you don't want to invite trouble by carrying too much cash around, and for another, the rate is usually better overseas. Take traveler's checks, dollars, and just enough foreign currency to see you through until you can get to an exchange at your destination. (Figure on one night's accommodations and two meals, in case the exchange is closed when you arrive.)

Deak International Group is the world's largest foreign-exchange organization. The best place in the United States to buy foreign currency is at one of their forty offices, since they deal in money from more than 120 countries. There is no service charge on currency transactions up to $350. You can even order currency by mail. For a list of services and free travel tips, send a stamped, self-addressed envelope to Deak and Co., 29 Broadway, New York, NY 10011, 212-635-0515.

Getting the Best Deal for Your Dollars

You can swap dollars for local currency in a number of places. Here are the most common, ranked according to how good a deal they will give you.

Exchange Shop/Cambio/Wechsel/ Bureau de Change

Usually, an exchange shop away from the airport or train station is the best place to buy the coin of the realm. It will offer you the best rate, and you can buy as much or as little money as you wish without pressure from salespersons.

Limit your loss on exchange.

All exchanges and banks post the sales and purchase prices of the currencies they sell. If the difference between the two prices for the dollar is more than about 5 percent, you can probably do better somewhere else. If converting from one currency to another is difficult for you, purchase a small calculator to do the job. (Special foreign-exchange calculators can be purchased, but they're hardly necessary since most conversion calculations can be performed easily on a standard calculator.)

Banks

The difference between banks and money-exchange shops is that changing money is *not* the primary business of a bank. A tourist in South America recently found that her money was worth twice as much in an exchange shop as in a local bank.

Hotels, Restaurants, and Shops

You can usually buy local currency at your hotel's main desk. Local shops and restaurants (particularly those near airports or international borders) will often take dollars, currency from neighboring countries, traveler's checks, credit cards, or personal checks. Expect to pay a premium for the privilege.

How Much Currency Should You Buy?

Wherever you are, don't buy too much. Because currency exchange does involve a fee to the bank, you will lose money trading dollars for francs, then francs for lira. It's better to buy a little bit less than you need than to buy too much. (You can always slip into a bank and change a ten-dollar bill.)

What to Do with Coins

Exchanges and banks do not exchange coins, so don't let yourself get loaded up with change from your purchases. Short of throwing it away, there are several ways to get rid of change.

Tips

Waitresses, maids, rest-room attendants, tour guides, and hotel employees expect some sort of gratuity. Get rid of your change by giving it to someone who can use it.

Do not tip too heavily. At many European restaurants, the tip is included in the bill (ask when you come in, if you want to be sure), so you should limit yourself to rounding up. In China, gratuities are considered an insult to the person who has provided the service. In other countries, especially East Germany and Israel, U.S. currency is so desirable that you will be disappointing those who wait on you if you give them a tip in their own money. The best policy is to ask your travel agent, tour guide, or hotel concierge what is acceptable.

In China, gratuities are considered an insult.

Give It Away
Spare change makes a nice gift to children. You can save it to bring home for nieces and nephews, or you can pass it out to the children of people you have met during your stay—if you are certain that it will not offend their parents. How about saving enough for your entire class?

Spend It
Hunt down that little Italian-ice shop you've passed three times a day and give yourself a treat, or save all of your coins and buy a bunch of postcards.

Make It into a Souvenir
A collection of foreign coins makes a unique bracelet, necklace, or tie tack. Some ingenious people have even set coins into plastic for use in decorative paperweights, clocks, bar tops, and coffee tables.

TRAVELER'S CHECKS

Traveler's checks are the simplest way to carry money while overseas. You can purchase traveler's checks from many sources, including your personal bank, American Express, and Thomas Cook. The cost generally runs around 1 percent of the total amount. Deak International and Barclay's Bank offer them at no cost.

Sometimes you get a better exchange rate for traveler's checks.

When deciding which type of traveler's checks to obtain, consider how widely this type is accepted and how many offices the company has overseas, in case your checks are lost or stolen and must be replaced.

Note: in some countries you will get a better rate of exchange for traveler's checks than for cash.

CREDIT CARDS AND PERSONAL CHECKS

Credit Cards

Major credit cards such as MasterCard, Visa, American Express, and Diner's Club are accepted wherever tourists are common.

Credit cards and checks may save you money.

It's worth asking whether a store or restaurant accepts credit cards because, surprisingly, you may actually save money by using one. First, you receive an extremely favorable rate of exchange when you charge something that must be paid for in foreign money. Second, if the dollar is rising in value, the delay between your purchase of an object priced in lira or yen and the transaction that charges you dollars for it may end up giving you an even better rate of exchange. Third, charges made in foreign countries take a long time to process, so they're like interest-free loans for the month or so until you get the bill. The fact that the store may charge you a small fee for the privilege of using a credit card is offset by all these benefits.

Personal Checks

You're probably so used to getting the third degree every time you try to pay by check at local stores that you'd never expect that it would be easy to use your personal checks overseas. But it is—so easy, in fact, that you wonder if these people *know* about the dangers of accepting checks.

Naturally, hotels, the offices of credit card companies, and American Express offices will cash checks for you if you're a customer. What's amazing is that so many places of business—from tiny little tourist traps to the most upscale boutiques—will take a personal check *without asking for identification.* (There ought to be a warning in this for you to watch your checkbook. If *you* can cash a check this easily, so can a pickpocket.)

Always inquire whether a business will take your personal check and what rate they offer. Generally speaking, you will not get the rate breaks you enjoy with dollars or credit cards. Checks written overseas do, however, take a long time to come floating back to your bank account.

WHEN TO TAKE DOLLARS

Although many countries, such as Canada, will accept dollars at an unfavorable rate, shopkeepers and roadside vendors in countries where inflation is high prefer dollars. Take a good supply of dollar bills to Mexico, Israel, and Egypt to bargain for small souvenirs such as postcards, religious figurines, and jewelry.

Factories in Germany, France, and Italy that specialize in selling seconds to Americans often give better exchange rates for dollars than banks do. It pays to ask if a store will take dollars and, if so, what their rate of exchange is.

GETTING CASH IN AN EMERGENCY

Inside the United States, your friends or family can bail you out of a financial emergency by wiring money through Western Union. You can have the cash in your desperate little hands within fifteen minutes if you wait in the office; it takes a little longer (and costs more) if the transaction involves delivery of the funds to you. Your financial savior can use MasterCard or Visa to send the money. The limit is usually about $2,000.

Emergency money in 15 minutes.

Overseas, you can have traveler's checks or cash cabled to you in care of a bank or agency, such as American Express. The delivery time is two days from the time you request the money. Expect to pay a surcharge for overseas service. If your situation is less urgent, have an American Express Money Order mailed to you. It's guaranteed, can be cashed immediately, and costs less to send than a cable.

You can arrange a transfer of funds overseas through a foreign branch of your bank, or use your ATM card to draw out cash. The availability of these services varies from bank to bank, so check with your bank before you head overseas.

Visa and MasterCard allow you to get a cash advance on your card at any bank displaying the Visa or MasterCard logo. Be warned, however, that this is one of the most expensive ways to get cash. You will be charged a transaction fee plus interest on the amount from the date of the transaction. With some credit-card issuers, the extra costs can add up to as much as *60 percent* of the amount you withdraw.

TELEPHONE CALLS

A call made from a hotel telephone can cost up to six times as much as it would if made from a pay phone. Always inquire about surcharges and rates *before* picking up the receiver. It's probably wisest to use a pay phone.

In Europe, pay phones are often available in the local post office. The clerk assigns you one of several telephone cubicles where you can make your call. After your conversation is completed, you pay the clerk the proper amount. This system saves you the bother of keeping track of a handful of foreign coins to feed the telephone.

Calling Collect

Phone the U.S. collect.

In most foreign countries it's expensive to use the telephone. The cheapest way to phone home from abroad is to call collect. Collect telephone calls are billed at the stateside rate, which runs about half the lowest overseas rate.

Telephone Credit Cards

If you don't want to impose on family or friends, obtain a telephone credit card from your local phone company and charge it to your home number. It's not cheap, but it's hardly as expensive as that bedside phone in the hotel room. Ask your telephone company for the booklet explaining how to avoid high surcharges on overseas calls.

EATING ON THE CHEAP

Even in the most expensive cities in the world, you can eat reasonably cheaply if you head for the places where the working class eats. The fare will likely be plain but nutritious . . . and nobody rushes you out the door when you finish your meal.

Got a yen for cafeteria food? All through Europe you can eat cheaply but well, at the local university cafeterias. Look for signs that say "MENSA." In locales as various as Paris and Israel, large cafeterias are traditional places for students to hang out. When your feet are weary from miles of sightseeing, drop in on one of these cafeterias and watch the people.

Pay less to dine, and have fun people-watching.

In Italian cities—especially expensive Venice—a tax is charged on food that is eaten while you are sitting down. Dine for half-price in Italy by having lunch at the little stand-up bars you will find everywhere.

Many cafés offer outside service. If it's atmosphere you want, go ahead and enjoy the pleasures of sitting at a little table and watching the locals and tourists—but be aware that it may be cheaper to eat indoors at the same restaurant.

Many foreign governments require restaurants to offer a daily tourist menu with fixed prices. In other places, a set menu serves about the same purpose. Generally, no substitutions are allowed when you order one of these meals. While you'll lose the flexibility of ordering anything you want, you can obtain a selection of national dishes at savings that can run as high as 20 percent.

Absolutely nothing is better than the locally made bread, wine, beer, cheese, and cold cuts sold in those little shops in small towns. Every region has its specialties. Be adventurous. You can stop at a bakery, a butcher shop, and a grocery store (for liquid refreshment), and eat like a king on a peasant's budget. One of the reasons this stuff tastes so great is that it doesn't have any preservatives in it, so it's best to buy fresh food every other day or so.

Local specialties with no preservatives.

SHOP 'TIL YOU DROP

If you pick up one of those shopping books—the kind with titles like *Great Shopping Bargains of the Western World*—you'll find that the author's idea of a bargain may be more like Princess Di's than yours. Unless you're an extremely well-paid teacher, you won't be looking for too many designer dresses, Italian loafers, or sets of hand-sewn underwear.

Seconds Shops and Outlets

Porcelain for a pittance.

The real places for bargains are seconds shops and factory outlets, where imperfect porcelain, wicker, crystal, toys, woolen goods—you name it—are sold for a comparative pittance. Some are associated with factories (for example, the porcelain factories in Kups, West Germany, or the famous English city of Stoke-on-Trent), while others are run by middlemen. You can load up on Capo di Monte flowers in Italy, Lladro figurines in Spain, and Royal Copenhagen sparrows in Denmark. If you evaluate the quality of the seconds carefully, nobody will ever know that you didn't pay full price.

Seconds shops are sometimes greatly ballyhooed, sometimes totally ignored in the literature put out by the local equivalents of chambers of commerce. The *best* way to find out about factory-seconds shops in the areas you will be visiting is to ask someone who lives there or who has lived there, a military friend or teacher living overseas, if you know of one. They will probably know where many local bargains can be found. *Don't* ask your tour guide, taxi driver, or any of the hotel staff—they're often paid by local merchants to steer tourists their way.

If your destination is Germany, it's worth it to get a copy of *Shopper's Guide to Germany,* by Dick and Vicki Johns. This is an outstanding compendium of factory outlets, antique stores, and flea markets, complete with excellent directions. Order it (for $8.95, plus $2 for postage) from Penn Books, 2280 E. Zermatt Circle, Sandy, Utah 84093.

Let's Make a Deal

In less industrialized regions, haggling is the favorite sport. Bargain hunters love to play the game at the bazaars in exotic Middle Eastern cities and elsewhere. Go ahead, haggle for your souvenirs—but be careful not to let yourself get too caught up in the thrill of it all. Purchase only what you want . . . and don't let the vendor know you really want it. Walk away if the price isn't exceptionally good. The vendor won't starve, and there are very few items in the average street-side stall that can't be found at another one around the corner.

In the Far East, beautiful gems and custom-made clothing can be purchased for a song. Indulge yourself, but remember that you must pay customs on purchases over $400. If your new suit can't be ready by the time you leave and must be mailed to you, you will pay duty on the full value of the suit.

It's easy to purchase furs, bone or horn jewelry, and other animal products overseas. However, if your new coat or necklace is made from an endangered species, it will be confiscated if you try to bring it into the U.S., and you may also be fined. Examine animal products carefully before you buy, and be aware of the restrictions on them. The vendor might not admit that they're from endangered species. Proceeding with caution will save you possible financial loss and will discourage the exploitation of species that are in danger of extinction.

Discourage the exploitation of endangered species.

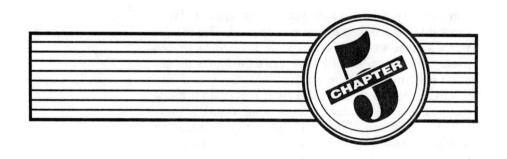

Travel with Class

Either you love it or you don't.

There is nothing halfway about traveling with students. It doesn't matter whether you're taking a trip around the world to see the Great Wall of China, or just across town to visit the local nature museum. Either you love it, or you don't. And the students, no matter what age group they are, seem to know whether you really enjoy being with them.

SURVIVING A WEEKEND (OR LONGER!) WITH THIRTY YOUNGSTERS

It's really not as hard as you might think. Surprisingly, junior-high students are often the easiest to travel with in groups. They are high-spirited and fun, yet old enough that they aren't prone to the tears and fatigue that smaller children are.

You can relax and enjoy your charges more by keeping a few simple guidelines in mind.

Make sure there are no surprises.

• *Keep order.* Legally, you stand in the place of a parent on an outing, and you should not allow

74

the students to run wild. Have a little talk before leaving, emphasizing the behavior you expect from students as fine as yours. You, as a representative of the school, are required to enforce school-district policy, such as rules against smoking. Let your students know this in advance, so there are no surprises.

Be vigilant, but avoid turning into a dragon. You are not the only chaperone. Arrange a schedule to make certain that everyone is safely in his or her room (if not sleeping) reasonably close to the appointed hour, that nobody is left behind when the bus takes off from a rest-room stop, and that at the end of the trip the students still have all the personal property they started out with.

• *Be prepared for minor emergencies.* Pack a first-aid kit that includes feminine-hygiene products, Band-Aids, and plenty of tissue. A roll of paper towels always comes in handy, and you can't imagine the uses you will come up with for trash bags.

• *Schedule with children in mind.* Allow plenty of milling-around time on stops to eat or to use the rest room. Children take a little more time than you might expect to get on and off a bus, make their way into a restaurant, order their food, and eat. Rest rooms need at least one adult security check during the stop. Children need to stretch their legs and exercise their vocal cords, too—so expect a little shrieking and running if you're traveling with younger children.

• *Have enough chaperones.* How many chaperones? Seldom does a trip have too many chaperones, especially with older children. Try to get parent volunteers. On the average, you will need one adult for every ten children, more or less. Some bus companies offer reduced fares for chaperones.

In Case of Emergency

One of the best features of an organized tour is that all the legalities are taken care of. Every traveler's application contains a release allowing medical treatment in case of emergency. Tour companies carry both medical and liability insurance to back you up if one of your charges becomes ill or is injured.

And if something goes wrong, you won't be alone. Tour companies that specialize in school-age groups maintain a trained staff in each place you visit. Tour representatives will help you make such decisions as whether to hospitalize a young patient or fly him or her home for treatment.

EDUCATIONAL TOURS IN THE U.S.

The major charter used for tours inside the United States—such as the perennial eighth-grade trip to Washington, D.C.—is Lakeland Tours, 2000 Holiday Drive, Charlottesville, VA 22901, 804-974-4321. Lakeland will make the arrangements for accommodations, travel, and admission, but you must plan your itinerary and be familiar with what is available.

The International Visitors Information Service (IVIS), a nonprofit community organization, will help you set up tours in the Washington, D.C. area at no charge. Contact Meridian House International, 733 15th Street, NW, Suite 300, Washington, D.C. 20005, 202-783-6540.

TOURS ABROAD

Harwood Tours

This company, which has specialized in student tours to Europe for thirty years, will send you and a group of students on a summer tour. Select from several tours to London, Paris, or other European destinations. As a tour leader, you will travel free . . . and your responsibilities *do not* include preparing or presenting educational commentaries on the places you visit. The tour company provides knowledgeable guides in each country. Call Harwood Tours at 800-972-7665 for brochures and further information.

The American Institute for Foreign Study (AIFS)

Travel free with six students.

This institute is part of a publicly owned educational-services company dedicated to increasing international understanding through cultural exchange. AIFS offers custom-designed tours aimed at meeting the educational goals set by the teachers who will be accompanying the groups. You travel free with six full-paying participants, and you can accumulate points toward free trips. For a counselor handbook, contact AIFS at 19 Bay State Road, Boston, MA 02215, 800-825-AIFS.

According to the AIFS counselor handbook, a teacher arranging a tour should follow these six steps:

1. *Contact the AIFS representative in your area for information about the programs offered.* He or she will help you to set up and publicize meetings.

2. *Choose your trip* before *approaching potential group members.* If you allow students or adults to help you with this decision, you will be going as many places as there are travelers. Familiarize yourself with your destinations.

3. *Select potential travelers.* Let them (and their parents) know that you want them to go with you. Avoid troublemakers—you will be responsible for them once the trip has begun. Encourage popular students who are involved with school affairs (but who are not necessarily "A" students) to come along. They will attract other students.

   List the names of travelers you want to invite personally to an organizational meeting. (List four times as many as you want to come, since not everybody will be able to accept your invitation.) Then contact the students you have listed and extend your invitation. It's a smart idea to contact parents directly, since they will encourage their children to attend.

   Contact parents directly.

   Announce your intentions to hold the meeting. Put up posters in your classroom, and let other teachers know that you are going to be taking a student group abroad.

4. *Hold group meetings.* Schedule at least two meetings. The first should be for students only and should be aimed at generating enthusiasm and sparking fund-raising plans. Hold this kind of

meeting at school, immediately after the end of classes. The second meeting should be for teachers, parents, and students. Hold it in the evening, at school (if allowed) or in a private home or church.

At both meetings, describe what the trip abroad will be like. Talk about your tour operator and what your trip will involve. Be sure to explain the cost. At the second meeting, circulate a sign-up sheet. Be prepared to answer questions about the tour, the expenses, and the tour operator. Set up a deadline for deposits and applications.

6. *Publicize and promote your tour.* Send press releases to local publications. Include your name, address, and telephone number, the names of people in your group, and a summary of your tour plans.

Fund-Raising

For many tour groups, fund-raising is a necessary part of travel. Although it's always possible to hope for assistance from the Rotary, American Veterans of Foreign Wars, Knights of Columbus, or other such group, your likeliest bet will be candy or jewelry sales.

Candy sales, book fairs, bake sales, and catalog sales.

As the sponsor of a school activity, you will probably receive half a dozen bulletins each month advertising fund-raising activities. If not, look on the backs of student magazines, where such activities are often advertised. The easiest fund-raiser (and the least popular with other teachers) is candy sales. Your group orders boxes of candy from a distributor, with each student agreeing to sell one or more boxes. When all the boxes are sold, the student salesperson receives a commission (or the commission is applied directly to the cost of the tour), and the fund-raising committee pays for the candy. Problems can arise when students fail to pay for their candy, lose their money, or mix up the records that tell who has paid. You need to supervise this and all such fund-raising activities *very carefully* to insure that it isn't a bad experience for the participants. For this reason it's better to have two short sales than one long, drawn-out sale.

If you can gain the support of the whole school, especially the librarian, a book fair is an effective fund-raiser. It is particularly attractive, since it promotes reading and is usually a once- or twice-a-year event that lasts several days or a week, rather than a campaign that must be supervised throughout the school year.

Another common fund-raiser is the bake sale. It's seldom hard to sell all the baked goods the kids bring to school if you set up near the cafeteria at lunchtime. The only problem with bake sales is that they do not raise very much money, parents will have to buy the ingredients, and the participants can become tired of making cookies long before they have earned enough for the trip.

Yet other fund-raisers involve catalog sales for such items as jewelry, Christmas wreaths, or stationery. Student salespersons are issued catalogs with which to sell items to friends, family, and teachers. Catalog sales can be very successful, but because they involve waiting for an order to arrive, they take a great deal of time. Sometimes the product that arrives is not as attractive (or as large) as everyone thought it would be. It's a good idea to have actual samples, if possible.

Your Role Overseas

Once you and your group have taken off on your trip, your role will change. Now it's your enthusiasm and support that will be crucial to a successful tour. Since everything is organized, you can relax and enjoy yourself. After all, you really wanted to go on this tour, too!

After all, you really wanted to go on this tour, too!

Don't overreact to cultural differences. Help your students to accept the foreign environment and the inconveniences of travel. Discourage carping and negativism among your charges by being positive yourself.

Make sure your group members are participating in scheduled activities, and keep the activities on time. Help the tour staff to keep things in line, especially during room check at night. It's a lot easier to drift off to sleep when you know where everybody is.

If all this sounds a lot like being a sergeant in the army, take heart. Thousands of such tours have gone their way uneventfully and concluded with the only memories being happy ones. Taking these tours is like eating popcorn—you can't take just one!

SUMMER EMPLOYMENT WITH FOREIGN-STUDENT GROUPS

At least one group employs teachers during the summer as instructors and chaperones for foreign-student groups touring the United States. Your assignment will be to teach conversational English and perhaps fill the students in on American culture. Contact Joann Beard, 7492 Seabluff Dr., #197, Huntington Beach, CA 92648 for information on the International Pacific Asian Consortium (INTERPAC). INTERPAC has centers in Los Angeles, Seattle, Phoenix, Philadelphia, San Diego, San Francisco, New York, Washington, D.C., and Hawaii for visiting Asian students.

INTERPAC also offers an outbound program of home stay or hotel stay in Japan, Taiwan, Hong Kong, and Korea for American student groups. Teachers accompanying at least fifteen students receive the trip free. These tours are usually taken by special-interest groups, such as bands, drill teams, and choirs.

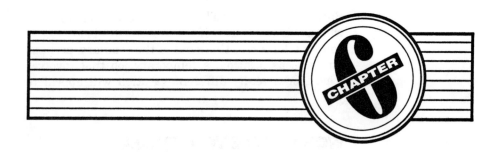

Special Interests

Who hasn't dreamed of combining the best of both worlds, education and travel? You could teach, go to school, or try something you've always wanted to do. Yet of all those teachers who have heard the call to Shangri-La, few have actually answered it.

Why? Well, to begin with, it's not easy to obtain information. If it's a job you're interested in, you have to know where to look for opportunities, and you must be persistent even to obtain an application. If you yearn for travel—anything from archaeological research to taking the kids on a barge cruise—it takes a little digging to unearth the details of when, where, and how much.

Then there are the qualifications. Are you educated enough? Are you physically fit? Do you teach the right subject, grade, or ethnic group? And there are the stories you hear in the teachers' lounge about the difficulties you might face. You *must* be adaptable and motivated to try something different.

You must *be adaptable and motivated to try something different.*

But, in the end, you'll need to decide for yourself whether travel that's off the beaten path is for you. If you long for a trip that's out of the ordinary, perhaps an overseas position, a temporary job that involves travel, or a really different vacation will appeal to you.

WORK WHILE YOU TRAVEL

Work Vacation

You won't get rich. If you're young and physically fit, unskilled summer work in another country is an excellent way to spend your vacation. You won't get rich—most of these jobs involve long hours and little pay—but you can expect to earn enough to pay for your room and board and your daily expenses. The main reward comes from getting to know the country and its people in a way tourists never can.

The work permit catch. However, getting a job overseas isn't as simple as stepping off an airplane and into an employment line. Most foreign governments want to make sure that their own people are employed before visitors are, and they don't want you to be a drain on their welfare system. For that reason, they require you to have a job before you can get a work permit. Unfortunately, few employers will hire workers who do not already have a work permit!

The way out of this frustrating dilemma is to obtain professional help. The Council on International Educational Exchange (CIEE), which annually helps more than a quarter of a million Americans go abroad, operates a program that cuts through the red tape for those who can prove they are students (a statement from your college that you are enrolled in a master's degree program should suffice). For about $82 CIEE will help students get a work permit for France, Germany, Great Britain, Ireland, New Zealand, Costa Rica, Jamaica, or Australia. The duration of the work permit varies with the country you select.

Along with the work permit, you will receive a list of possible employers, helpful information about living and working in that country, and assistance from a student organization in each country. It takes some time to get a work permit, so enroll in the program at least six weeks before you intend to leave the U.S. (For service within a week, CIEE recommends that you send your application by ExpressMail, enclosing $18 to cover the cost of return by ExpressMail.)

Work, Study, Travel Abroad was written by Marjorie Adolf Cohen and published by St. Martin's Press under the auspices of the Council on International Educational Exchange. This book contains full information on the program. Or you can obtain information by writing to Work Abroad Program, CIEE, 205 East 42nd Street, New York, NY 10017.

Volunteer Programs

Most countries outside the United States recruit volunteers for summer work camps, which may seem a little too grim for most Americans. But if you can't find any other way to go, perhaps you'd like to participate in reforestation, flood control, or school building in a country where your chances of finding an ordinary job are nil. The best source for information on this broad area is *Volunteer! The Comprehensive Guide to Voluntary Service in the U.S. and Abroad*. It can be ordered by mail from CIEE.

Teachers with master's degrees, one or two years of work experience, and knowledge of a second language can apply for a field position with United Nations Volunteers, a program that sends volunteers to countries that have requested their help. Volunteers usually stay for two years, training teachers, assisting refugees, or taking part in agricultural or mechanical projects. You must be sponsored by the Peace Corps. Write to the Peace Corps, Multilateral Programs, 806 Connecticut Avenue, NW, Room 701, Washington, D.C. 20525.

Travel with the Peace Corps.

The Peace Corps also places its own volunteers in sixty-two developing countries around the world. Skills in demand that teachers would be likely to possess include French-language, math or science, industrial arts, teaching, and agricultural skills. A hitch in the Peace Corps involves twelve to fourteen weeks of language training, plus two years as a volunteer. A living allowance is provided that equals a living wage in the host country, plus $175 a month (payable at the end of your service). Many Peace Corps volunteers use this accumulated living allowance to see the world on their way home. You can obtain an application for the Peace Corps from your local Peace Corps recruiter, or telephone the Peace Corps at 800-424-8580.

Archaeological Fieldwork

Find a dig where you'll get instruction.

If digging up ancient bones sounds to you like a great way to spend a holiday, you can easily get your wish. Old hands suggest that neophytes find either a field school or a dig where beginners are given instruction and supervision in correct archaeological procedure.

Two organizations publish listings of opportunities for volunteers at archaeological excavations. The Archaeological Institute of America (AIA) publishes the *Fieldwork Opportunities Bulletin,* which includes a bibliography listing important contacts. AIA also publishes *Archaeology* magazine, which includes in its semiannual travel issue a listing of excavations and archaeological sites that welcome visitors and volunteers. Write AIA at P.O. Box 1901, Kenmore Station, Boston, MA 02215 for current prices on these publications.

Archaeology Abroad, a British organization, publishes an annual bulletin and two newsletters listing excavations and archaeological opportunities. Contact the group's secretary for subscription information, enclosing a self-addressed envelope and international postal-reply coupons.

Other organizations offering similar expeditions for scientific purposes include Earthwatch, 10 Juniper Road, Belmont, MA 02178, 617-489-3030, and the University Research and Expeditions Program, University of California, 2223 Fulton Street, Berkeley, CA 94704, 415-462-6586. (See chapter 7 for circumstances under which your expenses may be tax-deductible.)

Long-Term Employment

Because of your special skills as a teacher, you're needed overseas. Many foreign governments and businesses, especially those in developing nations, need people to train teachers and to teach English and other vital subjects. Teachers with degrees in Teaching English as a Foreign Language (TEFL) or English as a Second Language (ESL) definitely have the advantage here.

In order to teach in another country, you need at least a bachelor's degree and two years' teaching experience. Expect to spend at least one to two years in your foreign teaching position. As in the United States, overseas schools begin looking for teachers in the spring.

Expect to spend at least one to two years in your foreign teaching position.

The educator who is thinking about seeking employment overseas should begin the search with a couple of helpful books. *Teaching Abroad,* available for $21.95 from the Institute of International Education, Box WW, 809 United Nations Plaza, New York, NY 10017, takes the reader step-by-step through the international maze. Listings include jobs for educators *outside* schools, working for industry or for educational associations.

Educator's Passport to International Jobs, by Rebecca Anthony and Gerald Roe, concentrates on the how-to aspects of international job-hunting. The book tells you how to find information, write résumés, evaluate job offers, prepare to live overseas, and—finally—plan for your return home. It's available for $9.95 from the publisher, Peterson's Guides Inc., 166 Bunn Drive, Box 2123, Princeton, NJ 08540.

The Department of Health and Human Resources offers the pamphlet *American Students and Teachers Abroad* to provide information about overseas study, teaching, work, and travel. Send $1 to the Superintendent of Documents, U.S. Government Printing Office, Washington, D.C., 20402, and ask for stock number 1780−01377.

There are two sorts of schools that hire American teachers: those with American students, and those with students from the host country and other foreign countries. The salaries they offer range from subsistence level to about what you'd receive from an American school district. The following paragraphs tell you where to apply for overseas teaching jobs.

Department of Defense Dependent Schools (DoDDS)

The DoDDS runs 220 schools.

The largest school district in the world is run by the Department of Defense for the purpose of educating the children of U.S. military and civilian personnel overseas. The system runs 220 elementary, junior-high, and high schools in twenty countries. Applicants must be credentialed teachers with several years of experience, willing to accept "any assignment to any location throughout the world where a vacancy exists and where their services are needed," according to the application.

No matter where you're asked to work, be prepared for culture shock. It's estimated that 30 percent of the teachers hired for DoDDS positions get off the plane, take one look at the place they've been assigned to, and go back home. However, in most ways working for DoDDS is very much like working in the United States. The salary is competitive, and the working conditions and holidays are about the same (except that you are also granted one free trip home every two years). And the choices of where to go on your holidays are incredible: how about visiting Tunisia over Thanksgiving, and Greece over Presidents' Day weekend?

DoDDS annually prints somewhere in the neighborhood of 6,000 applications for 1,000 job openings. When the applications are gone, you're out of luck until next year, so request yours early. Contact the Department of Defense, Office of Dependent Schools, Recruitment and Assignment Section, 2461 Eisenhower Avenue, Alexandria, VA 22331.

Private Organizations

If working with the military doesn't appeal to you, you can contact one of several private organizations that assist in placing educators overseas. The European Council of International Schools (ECIS) seeks educators at preuniversity levels for its 250 affiliated schools, most of which are in Europe. Certification and experience requirements may be slightly less rigorous than for the DoDDS system. Each fall, ECIS publishes an annual directory describing member schools and listing more than 500 other English-speaking independent schools worldwide. The *Directory* is available for $16.50, including airmail postage, from ECIS, 21B Lavant Street, Petersfield, Hampshire, England GU32 3EL.

The International Schools Service (ISS) finds teachers for more than 300 elementary and secondary American and international schools in Africa, Europe, the Middle East, the Far East, Latin America, and Southeast Asia. These schools are attended by the children of English-speaking businesspeople and diplomats. There is a $50 registration fee for applicants, and a further fee if you are placed in a position. All application documents should be completed and returned to ISS by late December for placement the following school year. For registration materials and information, write to ISS, 13 Roszell Road, P.O. Box 5910, Princeton, NJ 08543.

The ISS needs teachers for 300 schools.

The United Church Board for World Ministries recruits teachers of all denominations for high schools in Turkey, Japan, China, Zimbabwe, South Africa, and India. Assignments are for three years. Contact Personnel Secretary, United Church Board for World Ministries, 475 Riverside Drive, New York, NY 10115.

There are more than 1,000 English-language–oriented schools and colleges in about 150 countries that hire American teachers and administrators. Knowledge of a foreign language is seldom required. Openings are available on all levels and in most fields. Salaries are usually competitive with those in the U.S. For more information, contact Friends of World Teaching, P.O. Box 1049, San Diego, CA 92112, 619-275-4066.

As mentioned earlier, if you can teach English as a foreign language, you have the best chance for employment overseas. An organization called Teachers of English to Speakers of Other Languages (TESOL) publishes a bimonthly list of job openings for teachers trained in that field. Most positions require a master's degree and experience in teaching ESL.

Send $15 for the listing ($7.50 if you are a TESOL member) to TESOL, 1118 22nd Street, NW, Washington, D.C. 20037.

Overseas Employment Agencies
Be wary of overseas employment agencies that require substantial fees for their services. All too often their grandiose promises fade into nothing as soon as they have your check. It pays to read advertisements very carefully and to get a written agreement that specifies exactly what services you will receive.

Teacher-Exchange Programs
The U.S. Information Agency operates a teacher-exchange program that provides teaching assignments for elementary- and secondary-school teachers and for college instructors and professors. Candidates must have at least a bachelor's degree and three years of teaching experience. (In some cases, applicants must also have facility in the language of the host country.)

Most assignments are for a full academic year, and participating countries include Argentina, Australia, Belgium, Brazil, Canada, Colombia, Denmark, France, West Germany, Iceland, Italy, Luxembourg, the Netherlands, Norway, Panama, South Africa, Switzerland, and the United Kingdom. Applications must be received by October 1 for the following school year. Request the booklet *Opportunities Abroad for Educators* for details of positions open in the current year. Contact the Fullbright Teacher-Exchange Branch, E/SX, USIA, 301 Fourth Street, SW, Washington, D.C. 20547.

Live with host families while you teach.

AFS Intercultural Programs, founded in 1947, offer teachers a chance to live with host families in Asia, Latin America, and the Soviet Union while teaching or studying in an exchange that ranges from three weeks to one year. Most of the programs are aimed at language and social-studies teachers with secondary credentials, but teachers trained in other areas may be eligible to apply.

In Argentina, Chile, Costa Rica, Peru, and Thailand, the AFS exchange teachers serve as language and cultural resources in local schools. Through their involvement with the community, the host family, and the school, the teachers learn firsthand about other cultures. The one-year program in China is an academic one, focusing on Chinese language and culture, with the exchange teacher instructing Chinese university students in English. For more information on these exchange programs contact AFS at 313 East 43rd Street, New York, NY 10017, 800-AFS-INFO.

The Faculty Exchange Center, established in 1973 to help college professors who wanted to trade places for a time, operates like one of those trade-your-home-for-a-vacation groups. For a fee (currently $15) your name and qualifications will be listed in a catalog sent to other teachers. This group also runs a home exchange for teachers. Write to FEC, 952 Virginia Avenue, Lancaster, PA 17603 for details.

The National Faculty Exchange, 4656 West Jefferson, Suite 140, Ft. Wayne, IN 46804, also helps arrange teacher exchanges inside the U.S.

Tutoring Child Actors

A colleague living in Los Angeles answered an advertisement in a local newspaper several years ago and lucked into a position tutoring children on the sets of television shows and motion pictures. According to child-labor laws, child actors must be provided with tutors to carry on their studies when dramatic assignments require them to be away from school.

Judy Garland and Mickey Rooney were among the child actors educated at the "Little Red Schoolhouse" at the motion-picture studios during the 1930s. Today, independent producers are responsible for seeing that their young actors receive the education mandated by law. Such on-the-set tutorials usually involve a small number of usually well-behaved children, who are following a curriculum provided by their "home" school. Occasional opportunities arise to travel with your charges to location shoots, which can be anywhere in the world.

Travel to location shoots.

If this sounds glamorous and exciting to you, there are two catches. First, getting one of these jobs is very difficult, and second, if the actors don't work, neither do you. If the television series is canceled or the actors go out on strike, you can lose your job.

According to the personnel office at Universal Studios, applicants for tutoring positions should approach the independent production companies. Submit your résumé, including your work experience and the type of teaching credentials you hold, to each production company with which you would like to work.

The *Pacific Coast Studio Directory* contains a complete listing of Los Angeles production companies and directors, along with their addresses and telephone numbers. For a year's subscription, send $20 to 6313 Yucca St., Hollywood, CA 90028.

Cruise Ships

Cruise lines that specialize in family packages have openings for personnel who are qualified to care for and entertain children, although many of these positions are filled overseas. Carnival Cruise Line's job line (800-327-7373) lists "child counselor" as a position for which the company recruits applicants. Send your résumé along with pertinent information to Carnival Cruise Line, 5225 NW 87th Avenue, Miami, FL 33178-21893, Attn.: Steve Petrosky.

LEARN WHILE YOU TRAVEL

Deduct educational travel from your taxes.

Travel is especially relevant for those in the teaching profession. You can teach map skills for forty years, but one summer spent exploring South America may teach you more about international boundaries than all the in-service training you've had in your whole career.

School districts recognize the benefits of travel, and they usually encourage it by allowing sabbatical leaves and other programs that give teachers a chance to see the world. Uncle Sam and his tight-fisted cousin, the IRS, recognize how valuable it is, too, and allow you to deduct some of the costs of educational travel from your taxes.

Local College Courses

The first place to look for educational travel is in brochures from your local community college. In recent years such colleges have blossomed into a veritable flowerbed of cultural opportunity, including many travel programs.

Every semester, community colleges offer a wide array of classes involving travel near or far. You can, for example, visit the wine country of California, watch whales along the coast, see the fall foilage in the Northeast, or take a tour of Mazatlán. These tours are all just for the sheer pleasure of travel.

University Travel Courses

So many travel courses, so little time! You don't have to wade through a stack of brochures from a hundred colleges and universities to find the travel course that's right for you. *World Study and Travel for Teachers* lists 240 travel-study programs sponsored by ninety-two different institutions. Check out the array of independent-study programs and trips for credit. The subject areas are wide-ranging, including foreign languages, science, social studies, and the arts. Send $4 to AFT Order Department, 555 New Jersey Ave., Washington, D.C. 20001, 202-879-4424.

So many travel courses, so little time!

Learning to speak Spanish or German is a lot easier in the countries where these languages are the native tongue. A four-week program can be as low as $500, not including airfare. To sign up for language studies in connection with home stays in Japan, Canada, France, West Germany, Portugal, Italy, Costa Rica, or Spain, contact Language Studies Enrollment Center, P.O. Box 5095, Anaheim, CA 92814, 714-527-2918.

Even the NEA is getting into the act with a symposium at Britain's prestigious Oxford College, titled "NEA/Oxford Symposium: Oxford and the Education System Today." Stroll through the magnificent university town of Oxford, hobnob with British and American colleagues, and attend lectures on the British education system. You even get to stay in "student digs" (traditional student apartments similar to the ones members of the British royal family lived in during their university days) and dine in Oxford's centuries-old Great Hall. Contact NEA Special Services, National Education Association, 1201 16th Street, NW, Washington, D.C. 20036.

Stroll through Oxford.

Create your own travel-study program.

You can earn between one and four credits in a travel-study course of your own devising in a program offered by Vermont's Goddard College. Studying specific aspects of American or foreign cultures and meeting course objectives by maintaining an academic log or project journal may qualify most of the expenses as tax-deductible. (Check with your tax adviser for the final word on this before you make the plunge.) Contact James Galloway, Campus Administrator, Travel for Academic Growth, Goddard College, Plainfield, VT 05667, 802-454-7835 or 802-454-8311. For information on a similar program, contact Steven Tash, Travel/Study Program, University of California Extension, P.O. Box 16501, Irvine, CA 92713, 714-586-8992.

Other Options

There's something for everyone in *Vacation Study Abroad*, available for $16.95 from Publications Service, Institute of International Education, 809 United Nations Plaza, New York, NY 10017. More than 2,200 programs for participants ages five through seventy-five are listed, along with the specifics of costs, housing, dates, locations, and deadlines.

TRAVEL WITH A TWIST

Tourists have more vacation options today than ever before. Perhaps you'd like to vacation on an Indian reservation . . . cycle across the United States . . . or track down the missing members of your family tree. All of these options, and more, are possible.

The Great Outdoors

If the great outdoors is just your style, send for a free booklet on hiking trails and facilities from National Science and Recreational Trails, National Park Service, Dept. of the Interior, Washington, D.C. 20240. To find out about camping and hiking on private property, contact the American Forest Institute, 1619 Massachusetts Ave., Washington, D.C. 20006.

Under Starry Skies is a free listing of 300 dude

ranches, Western outdoor resorts, river-rafting companies, and bed-and-breakfasts in five Western states. For those whose childhood idol was Roy Rogers, this is your big chance to live out your fantasies. Contact Central Resort Report, P.O. Box 979, Sun Valley, ID 83353.

Perhaps you'd like to share the Old West with Native Americans. Some Indian reservations welcome tourists. If you'd like to sightsee with an Indian guide, contact Phoenix Indian Center, 333 Indian School Road, Phoenix, AZ 85031.

Vacation on a reservation.

Biking

If you'd rather travel on two wheels than four, consider taking a cycling trip. There are two types to select from. Organized cycling excursions, available all over North America and Europe, are guided by leaders who set the itinerary, arrange for accommodations, and lead the way. If you like to cycle in a group that may be competitive and you enjoy the idea of having your gear carried in a support vehicle, this is the biking holiday for you. Many major universities, such as the University of California, offer cycling tours here and abroad. The travel sections of large newspapers frequently carry listings of bicycle tours and numbers to call to join them. Another source of information on bicycle tours is *Bicycling* magazine, which is available free at bicycle stores specializing in imported bikes.

On the other hand, those who prefer a comfortable group of friends and the opportunity to smell the flowers along the way, can easily organize their own cycling tour. All it takes is between two and six like-minded people, each with a good bike (and current passport, if you are going overseas), an adventuresome spirit, and an energetic set of legs. If foreign cycling is to your taste, bikes are easily handled in bike boxes on major airlines, and most European railroads are happy to accommodate bicycles in their baggage cars, often for free. Experienced touring cyclists suggest that novices research the availability of bike parts in all of the countries they plan to visit. It's wise to take spare parts and to include a willing bike mechanic in the group.

Organize your own tour.

Travel with a Twist

For more information on bicycle tours and on bicycling in general, pick up a copy of *Bicycle Guide* (Raben Publishing Company, 711 Boylston St., Boston, MA 02116) or *Bikereport* (Bikecentennial, Inc.). The cost of this magazine is $2.50. The Bicycle Travel Association, Box 8303, Missoula, MT 59807, will send you a free information packet, and your local bicycle shop should have some pertinent suggestions as well.

Genealogical Research

Tracking down your family tree is a meaningful way to spend a holiday. Ever since Alex Haley wrote *Roots*, Americans have been visiting their ancestral homes to find long-lost relatives and to see what it was really like "back there."

During the period when a flood of emigrants rushed from Europe to the United States, most major ports kept records of those who passed through them, including their cities of birth. These old records still exist. With a little detective work, you can write for them, then arrange a trip to your family's hometown.

Visit your ancestors' hometown.

Several countries have set up special offices to assist people who are researching their ancestors or relatives. For information about family members who emigrated from Ireland, contact the Irish Ancestral Research Foundation, Barleymount, Kilarney, County Kerry, Ireland, or the Hibernian Research Company, Limited, Windsor House, 22 Windsor Road, Rathmines, Dublin 6, Ireland. In France, contact the Archivs des Champes Syngicales de Genealogites, 18 Rue de Cherche, Midi, Paris, France, telephone 1-45-48-5224.

Because Hamburg was the central embarkation point for European emigrants, records are maintained on many Eastern European nationalities, as well as Germans and Italians. The Historic Emigration Office in the Museum for Hamburg History will give you information about relatives who immigrated through the port of Hamburg if you can supply their names and the year they left for North America. (Write to: Historic Emigration Office, Museum of Hamburg History, Hamburg, West Germany.)

SPECIAL CHALLENGES

Traveling with Disabilities

There's help for families whose vacation plans include someone who is handicapped, elderly, or ill. *Access to the World*, by Louise Weiss (published by Facts on File), tackles the special problems faced by the disabled when they travel, such as boarding an airplane or ship, arranging for a wheelchair, staying comfortable during the trip, and taking a seeing-eye dog on board. Included are vacation ideas tailored for the disabled, listings of travel agents and tour operators that specialize in travel for the handicapped, and practical tips that enable physically challenged travelers to see the world and enjoy the trip.

If camping is your game, *Access Guide to the National Parks* provides information on what facilities and services are available for the physically handicapped in national park areas. To order, contact Consumer Information Center, Pueblo, CO 81009.

For information on train travel for persons confined to wheelchairs, write Amtrak Distribution Center, P.O. Box 311, Addison, IL 60101 and ask for the free brochure *Access*. Amtrak offers a 25 percent discount for handicapped passengers and senior citizens on fares over $40.

Greyhound Bus Lines, recognizing the problems faced by physically challenged people in traveling by bus, allows a companion/helper to travel free. The brochure *Helping Hand* is available at no charge at Greyhound depots or through Public Relations, Greyhound Tower, Mail Station 1810, Phoenix, AZ 85077.

Traveling with Kids

It used to be that most tours wouldn't take children, and on many cruises they were locked away all day in supervised areas. But now, after years of being neglected by the more sophisticated travel industry, children are beginning to come into their own. Hotels, tour operators, and cruise lines have begun to realize that parents want to spend quality time with their children while traveling. A recent poll showed that 10 percent of parents on *business* trips brought their youngsters along, too. Suddenly, vacations with children are back in vogue. From Club Med to the Ritz-Carlton, families are playing together.

Whether you set out to tour the world or merely to drive cross-country, plan your trip with your children in mind. Break up sightseeing and long car rides because young bodies get tired fast. A good compromise between adult and child is to see the museums and other "grown-up stuff" in the morning, and to spend the afternoon doing things like swimming and building sand castles, visiting an alligator farm, or playing arcade games.

For long trips, try purchasing small-but-entertaining items that can be kept in a grab bag. Your youngster will love pulling out a new toy each day. Limit these to small items, such as a deck of cards, a new book, or a toy airplane. Older children will also likely enjoy using inexpensive cameras. And if you have a youngster whose reading skills are shaky, turn him or her into the "navigator," with the job of reading road signs and maps.

A great book to take with you on your next vacation is *How to Take Great Trips with Your Kids*, by Sandford and Joan Portnoy (published by the Harvard Company). This book can help you with everything from settling squabbles between kids to finding a place to change a diaper.

Once you've made the decision to transform your daydreams into reality, you'll find that travel tailored to your personal interests and needs can be extremely rewarding.

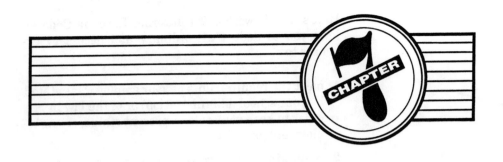

Making the Best of Taxing Situations

While educators no longer enjoy the generous tax deductions once granted them for travel, it's still possible to combine work with pleasure. This chapter contains the latest tips on how to save money on taxes when you travel. (Of course, tax situations vary from year to year and from individual to individual, so it's wise to get the assistance of your lawyer, tax adviser, or accountant before going out on a limb.)

INCOME-TAX DEDUCTIONS

As a result of the 1987 Tax Reform Law, teachers can no longer deduct travel for general educational purposes. However, the teaching profession still offers unique tax advantages for educators who travel, take courses, publish, attend seminars, or want to improve their skills.

Teaching offers tax advantages for educators who travel.

Here's how it works. The Internal Revenue Code allows you to deduct all ordinary and necessary expenses to

1. meet the requirements of your employer (as stated by your school administration) or of the law in order to keep your salary, present status, or employment, or

2. maintain or improve skills required to perform your duties as an educator.

How are you evaluated by your school district? In most instances you are expected to measure up in several areas, including organization of material, record keeping, relationship with faculty and students, classroom management, appearance, *publications, involvement in professional organizations, professional growth, and knowledge of your subject matter.* The last four criteria have important tax implications.

Basically, the government's rationale in granting tax deductions to teachers is that educators must constantly upgrade their skills to meet professional criteria of employment and advancement. To justify a tax deduction, teachers should be able to show the relationship between their outside educational activity and the requirements of their school districts for continued employment.

Upgrading or Maintaining Skills

Although you cannot deduct education that qualifies you for a new position (for example, coursework leading to a teacher's credential when you are not currently working in the classroom) you can deduct classes that keep you abreast of educational methods, teaching techniques, and your subject matter.

Research

Travel that is undertaken as part of research leading to publication can be deducted as a business expense. For example, if you are preparing a book or scholarly article on Etruscan tombs, you can deduct the cost of transportation, lodging, meals, camera film, business phone calls, reproduction, guides, and any fees involved in doing your research. Under certain conditions, your deductions may be limited to the amount of compensation you receive for the book or article.

Volunteering

Teachers who participate as active volunteers in research expeditions sponsored by nonprofit organizations are able to deduct food, travel, and other expenses.

Similarly, if you volunteer your service to national parks for such tasks as maintaining trails, assisting park rangers, and patrolling wilderness areas, your expenses are tax deductible. The National Forest Service Volunteer Program, Box 37483, Washington, D.C. 20013 can provide you with the details.

Deducting Travel Costs

According to IRS publication 508, you may deduct the cost of travel (normally including meals and lodging, if overnight) for educational travel if it is directly related to maintaining or improving your teaching skills, or to retaining your seniority or position on the pay scale. Such deductible travel falls into six categories: travel to obtain education, travel between jobs, travel to professional meetings, travel to seek employment, extracurricular travel, and sabbatical travel.

Six categories of deductible travel.

When you must be away from home overnight because of your work, you can ordinarily deduct all expenses—for example, transportation, lodging, meals, bus or cab fare, auto expenses, cleaning, laundry, professional telephone calls, and tips. (Be sure to pay by check or credit card for all items that might be tax-deductible.) If you are attending a seminar or convention, you may still deduct your transportation and other expenses, but only 80 percent of your meals are deductible. Keep programs, take notes on speakers, collect teachers' aids, and participate in presentations. Doing so not only proves your intent to Uncle Sam, it also improves your effectiveness as a teacher.

Travel over summer, winter, or spring break that is directly related to maintaining or improving your job skills is also deductible. Don't forget to deduct airfare, mileage, parking, turnpike tolls, camera film, classroom materials, passport, visas, vaccinations, baggage fees, charges for traveler's checks, and other travel-related expenses. You must be able to prove that your travel is necessary. For example, if you go to London to take an education course, your travel expenses are deductible only if such a course is not available elsewhere. Many universities offer courses tailored to meet this distinction. See chapter 6 for further information about such offerings.

Sabbatical Leave

Most of the travel expenses associated with sabbatical leave are tax deductible. As with other forms of educational travel, you will need to document the educational nature of your sabbatical. With your tax return, enclose a statement from your employer that the leave was granted for some educational purpose, along with a brief report containing your itinerary and a listing of people and educational resources you visited. Include dates and places.

Extracurricular Travel

Travel undertaken on behalf of your school outside of normal classes is tax deductible if you are not reimbursed by the school district. All those miles you've run up escorting the debating team or the journalism class to competitions and workshops can be deducted at the rate of twenty-four cents a mile.

There are many tax guides on the market; two that are of outstanding value to teachers are described here. *Educators Income Tax Guide* takes a workbook approach to taxes. This publication, which is tailored for teachers and is revised annually, includes tax tips, explanations of current income-tax laws, and sample forms. Especially helpful is the section on deducting travel expenses. You can obtain this invaluable guide from Teachers Tax Service, P.O. Box 1329, San Carlos, CA 94970. The 1989 cost is

$6.95, plus $1.95 for special handling and first-class postage.

Financial Tips for Teachers, by Alan Jay Weiss and Larry Strauss (published by Willowisp Press), the companion book to this series, is available through Willowisp Press. Coauthor Weiss is a tax consultant whose specialty is teachers and their tax situation. This handy book covers taxes, financial planning, and additional sources of income.

TAXES IN FOREIGN COUNTRIES

Import Duties

While you can't escape paying customs on articles above a certain value imported into the United States, many foreign countries—notably within the United Kingdom and Europe—will allow you to avoid import duties upon arrival. The limits on cigarettes, perfumes, and liquors vary from country to country, but generally speaking they are set high enough to allow for personal consumption during your visit. Check with a travel agent, airline, or national tourist office for the limitations of the country you intend to visit.

Avoid import duties in Europe.

Gifts

Although you may not want to use the duty-free articles mentioned above, consider bringing them with you as gifts. American goods are valued by people who reside in other countries, where high taxes make items we take for granted very expensive. Cigarettes, liquor, and perfume are especially popular, but canned nuts, English-language books (especially picture books of the U.S.), and scented soaps are also received with enthusiasm. If you are in doubt about your host's tastes, inquire in advance.

National Taxes

In countries anxious for tourist dollars—for example, Israel and the Commonwealth nations—it is possible to purchase such relatively expensive items as fur

Value-Added Tax.

coats, leather jackets, and Scottish kilts without paying the Value-Added Tax (VAT). The procedure differs from country to country, but it usually involves obtaining a special receipt at the time of purchase, having the article mailed to you at your home (yes, they *do* arrive), or picking your purchase up at the airport on your way home.

Because you will be required to pay U.S. Customs duty on anything mailed to your home, try to take your purchases with you. You will probably have to show your receipt, airline ticket, passport, and a special VAT form to a customs officer as you leave the country you are visiting. Not every store offers VAT refunds, so inquire before you shop.

DUTY-FREE SHOPPING

Gifts valued up to $50 sent to a friend by mail from overseas are not taxable. Mark the package "Unsolicited Gift." You will, however, be taxed on items you purchase abroad and have mailed to your home address, *whatever their value.*

Duty-free shops overseas do not necessarily save you money.

Duty-free shops overseas do not necessarily save you money. The best bargains they carry are cigarettes, liquor, and perfume, which may otherwise be heavily taxed at your destination. Be sure to keep everything in the distinctive "duty-free" bag the store provides.

Other items are usually not worth buying unless you're just flying through and want to pick something up—for example, a piece of Royal Copenhagen porcelain while you're in Copenhagen en route to Oslo. Keep in mind that airport shops are usually quite expensive—you can probably find something equally nice on your travels without worrying about paying duty.

Visiting a nearby country or U.S. territories can be an opportunity to buy liquor or handicrafts cheaply. If you cross into Mexico or Canada daily, you may bring home $25 worth of duty-free goods each day. All goods must be for your personal or household use. Less frequent visitors to our neighboring countries may bring back up to $400 worth of goods, but only once every thirty days. Vacationing in a U.S.

territory, such as Puerto Rico or the Virgin Islands? You will be allowed to bring back up to $800 worth of duty-free goods.

WHAT YOU MAY AND MAY NOT BRING INTO THE U.S.

U.S. Customs

There are limits to what you may bring with you when you return to the United States. Generally speaking, if you bring more than $400 worth of goods purchased elsewhere, more than one liter of alcohol, or more than $5,000 in currency or monetary instruments, you will have to pay customs. Cigarettes and perfume are also regulated.

If you intend to take expensive articles manufactured outside the U.S. with you on your trip (for example, a camera), it might be a good idea to preregister the serial numbers with the U.S. Customs office or to bring receipts with you. Customs officials have been known to levy duties on such items.

Some items are banned in the United States. Not surprisingly, you can't bring in drugs or firearms (including fireworks). But did you know that you are also not allowed to bring in tortoise-shell souvenirs, counterfeit items, or grapefruit? You may not bring any products made from endangered species into this country, *even though you may have been able to purchase them in countries you visited.* Trademark laws protect brand names such as Adidas and Gucci. If you bring home a cheap knockoff of a famous-name product, you can expect to have it taken away from you. Agricultural quarantine regulations forbid the importation of uninspected meat, vegetables, fruit, or plants.

Don't buy non-importable items.

You will be asked to declare anything of the above nature. Be honest, and surrender contraband if you have accidentally acquired it. These regulations are not simply arbitrary rules, and you will be fined if you are caught violating them.

It is your responsibility to know what can be brought into the U.S. and what can't. The best guide to current rules about customs is *Know Before You Go*, available from the U.S. Customs Service, Public Information, Room 201, 6 World Trade Center, New York, NY 10048, 212-466-5550. Ask for the travel pack if you'd also like information on mailing gifts from overseas and on liquor regulations.

The Department of Agriculture, Plant and Animal Health Inspection Service, 732 Federal Building, 6505 Belcrest Road, Hyattsville, Maryland 20782 offers a free pamphlet called *Traveler's Tips* (in English, Spanish, Japanese, and Italian), which should clear up any questions you might have about what food or plant products may be brought into the country.

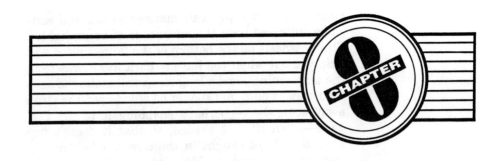

CHAPTER 8

Don't Leave Home Without Them

N ow, suddenly, it's the last minute. You've successfully planned your trip, found a travel agent, gotten all your documents in order, and . . . it's time to go. Before you shut the door for the last time, check to make sure you haven't forgotten anything. This chapter will help you to remember the things you can't leave home without.

It's time to go.

PACK UP YOUR TROUBLES

Luggage

Except for aesthetic reasons, it doesn't matter whether you have an expensive matched set of luggage or several pieces you rescued from a garage sale. There are, however, a few practical aspects to consider when buying luggage. You should try to limit yourself to what you can manage alone, and soft-sided suitcases have the advantage of being lighter. Sturdy wheels on the bottom of the largest piece will help you out when you have to park five blocks from the air terminal, and a long strap will make the suitcase easy to pull. You should be able to put the strap away somewhere—perhaps snapping it to the luggage—when it's not needed, so that it doesn't flop around and get caught in the conveyer belt on the way into the airplane. Make certain that your suitcase closes and *stays* closed and, preferably, that it locks. You don't want to arrive at the luggage pickup to find your unmentionables riding the conveyer all by themselves.

Remove old stickers and destination labels from your luggage.

Remove old stickers and destination labels from your luggage. Put something brightly colored—tape, a yarn pom-pom, or a travel sticker—near the handle to help you spot your suitcase on the luggage carousel. For security's sake, put your home address and telephone number, along with information on where you can be reached during your trip, on the *inside* of your luggage rather than on outside luggage labels. If your address is on the outside, clever thieves might spot it and use the opportunity to burglarize your home while you are on vacation. On outside luggage labels, give your name and address of destination only. Some travelers have their names and social security numbers engraved on their luggage, briefcases, and cameras.

You should also have a carry-on bag for items you can't do without.

You should also have a carry-on bag for items you can't do without. Be sure to keep with you your passport, your money (including traveler's checks and enough local currency to get you through the first night at your destination), and any medications you take regularly. That way you'll be secure if your larger luggage is delayed or lost.

Packing Tips

When you enter certain countries, such as Israel, you may be asked to click the shutter on your camera or squeeze a little toothpaste out of your toothpaste tube to show that the contents are innocuous, so have these items where you can reach them easily.

When packing tubes and bottles, put them in zip-lock plastic bags—they'll be easier to find in a crowded suitcase, and your clothing will be protected if any lids become loosened due to changes in air pressure. Zip-lock bags also make fine containers for many other items, such as jewelry, shoes, makeup, and children's toys, since they keep small items separate and protected.

Pack These In Carry-On Luggage, Briefcase, or Purse:

tickets
passport/visa
keys for house and car
driver's license
confirmation of hotel reservation
checkbook
credit cards (only those you intend to use)
some foreign currency (if traveling overseas)
traveler's checks
vaccination certificate
change for tips ($20 in dollar bills)
money belt or pouch
light slippers to wear while traveling
pocket-sized packages of facial tissues
pocket calculator (a must if going overseas)
film/computer disks (if not in a separate, lead-lined pouch)
medications you take regularly, and prescriptions for them
glasses prescription(s)
first-aid kit
    motion-sickness pills
    Pepto-Bismol™
    aspirin or other mild pain reliever
    feminine-hygiene products
    antibiotic cream
    lip salve
    a small container of skin moisturizer
    needle and white thread
    manicure scissors
    fingernail file
a list of the items packed in your regular luggage (in case it gets lost)

Pack These in Your Regular Luggage:

spare pair of glasses, if the trip will last more than a week
names, telephone numbers, and addresses of friends and family
names, telephone numbers, and addresses of people you intend to
  look up
clothing sizes of people for whom you plan to buy gifts
registrations or receipts for expensive possessions of foreign origin
  (such as fur coats, cameras, or watches)
itinerary
sunglasses
suntan lotion
bath soap in a container
shampoo
toiletries
lingerie soap for hand washables
receipts listing all ticket numbers and traveler's check numbers
a certified copy of your birth certificate (for obtaining a duplicate
  passport, if necessary)
extra set of photos (for a duplicate passport)
photocopy of your passport
umbrella
blow dryer
shaver
guidebooks/phrase books/foreign-language dictionaries
electric adapter or converter*
maps
travel-club cards
reading material/travel guides
travel alarm clock
flashlight
travel iron

If your exposed film is valuable, allow the security guards to hand-check the bag.

Film (including exposed film) should be packed separately so it doesn't have to go through X-ray machines. Some photographers swear by lead-lined film pouches; others swear they don't work. If your exposed film is valuable, allow the security guards to hand-check the bag.

*Electricity and electrical outlets in foreign countries differ from those in the United States. Before you travel, find out what types of adapters or converters you will need in the country you will be

Don't Leave Home Without Them

visiting. It may be worthwhile to invest in a hair dryer that uses direct current.

Security

Recent events have taught us to exercise caution when we are traveling. Because not everyone has motives as innocent as yours, always lock your bags, and don't let them out of your sight unless it's to put them in a luggage locker. Also, *do not* accept wrapped packages from anyone, however nice the person seems or how harmless the package appears. A small package could contain explosives timed to go off while you're aloft. If you see an unattended briefcase or suitcase in the train, airplane, or ship terminal, *report it to the authorities immediately.*

WHAT TO WEAR

Dress comfortably before you set out, whether you'll be traveling by car, boat, or plane. Keep in mind that the weather is likely to be different when you reach your destination from what it was when you left. Your shoes should be easy on your feet and not likely to slip on ramps or stairs. It's practical to bring some of the hard-to-pack items, such as your coat and sweater, with you. You can always stow them while you are traveling, and a coat makes an admirable blanket if the storage bins and coat closets are full.

While en route, loosen constrictive clothing. Many people change from shoes into soft slippers because their feet swell while traveling. Aboard airplanes, it's advisable to use lip salve and skin moisturizer because of the drying effect of the pressurized air in the cabin. Those who wear contact lenses should bring artificial-tears solution.

While en route, loosen constric-tive clothing.

BE SAFE, NOT SORRY

Plan from the beginning to save yourself worry by following these rules for hassle-free travel.

1. Keep some of your money separate from the rest for emergencies. Put your passport and most of your money in a little pouch that's worn around

Things to Do Before You Leave

- Label your luggage, both inside and out.

- Make a list of the items you've packed (for insurance purposes).

- Stop mail and newspaper deliveries.

- Arrange for someone to take in the mail (if not stopped), pick up circulars left on the doorstep, water your plants, feed your pets, check the house for leaks, and start your automobile once a week. Housesitters can be engaged for this purpose. Housesitting services will even buy milk and other basic supplies for your return.

- Arrange to have the lawn mowed and the yard kept up.

- Lock all doors and windows.

- Leave your itinerary with family or friends so you can be contacted in case of an emergency.

- Leave an extra set of house keys with a neighbor or family member so someone can get in if necessary.

- If you are going to be away for some time, pay your bills in advance and perhaps set up an automatic withdrawal for certain important payments (such as the mortgage).

- Let the police know that you will be away and that someone will be taking care of your house.

- Get rid of any food that might spoil while you are away.

- Empty the trash.

- In the winter, turn down the thermostat and winterize pipes and drains.

- Fix any leaky water faucets.

- Put all valuables and important documents in a safe place, such as a safe-deposit box or fireproof locked box.

- Purchase a timer to turn lights on and off so your house won't look empty.

- Don't close the blinds or pull down the shades—this will invite robbers.

your neck (you can buy such a pouch in a travel store); at night, you might sleep with it under your pillow. (This may sound paranoid—but just ask any embassy how many people have had their passports and money stolen while they slept!) But remember to retrieve it from under your pillow before you leave.

2. Put photostats of your important documents someplace different from the originals. The U.S. Passport Agency recommends that you keep a photocopy of your passport, two passport photos, and a certified birth certificate in your luggage just in case you need to replace your passport.

3. Never leave valuables unattended. While you're out, lock them in the hotel safe or keep them with you, not on your dresser.

4. Store bulky items and luggage in a locker at the train station or airport if you won't need them during this stopover. (It's a good idea to pack with this in mind.) Put valuables in the hotel safe.

5. Label everything—luggage, purse, coat, umbrella, sweater, camera, etc.—with your name and address. Again: do *not* put your home address on the outside of your luggage.

Label everything with your name and address.

6. Consider security when selecting your accommodations. Small pensions or Gasthauses that lock up at night are more secure than big, open hotels.

7. Stay away from deserted railway stations, airports, and bus stations at night.

IN CASE YOU RUN INTO TROUBLE

Outside U.S. borders, your cruise or tour operator is your best source of information. Most package operations have offices or representatives in the countries their tours visit. If you encounter problems with accommodations, money, or lost personal property, ask your "host" for assistance.

If you are robbed, mugged, or involved in an accident, contact the local police first. Use your camera to

Contact the local police first.

make a photographic record of any damage done. Next, call on the American consulate or embassy if you need assistance in dealing with police or lawyers, or if you need to replace your passport.

If you are arrested or detained by local authorities in a foreign country, ask to see a representative of the American consulate or embassy. He or she will negotiate with the authorities for your release, or—in the worst case—help you obtain a lawyer and contact your relatives back home if you are imprisoned.

Don't bring a salami into Norway.

The best way to avoid all this unpleasantness is to keep your wits about you. Have all the correct papers when crossing international borders. Try to avoid appearing nervous or in a hurry. (*All* of your luggage will be thoroughly searched if you arouse suspicion.) Be aware of the laws of countries you visit, and don't break them—not even in little ways, such as bringing a salami into Norway. (Yes, that's illegal! The rabies quarantines in Norway, Sweden, and Finland extend to meat products.)

In many countries, if you are arrested you are subject to a long and decidedly unfriendly judicial process. Treat local police officers and customs officials with respect, and your passage through their jurisdiction will be a happy one.

TO YOUR GOOD HEALTH

Jet Lag

Following a long flight, travelers are often felled by the exhaustion and sense of disconnectedness known as "jet lag." There are many explanations for jet lag, primary among them being that travel through several time zones disorients the body's internal clock. Other contributory factors may include: exhaustion before leaving, dehydration caused by the pressurized cabin, consumption of alcohol in flight, or failure to drink enough fluids, and overeating or eating the wrong kinds of foods. Many tours routinely include a day of rest after a long flight to give tourists a chance to recuperate. It's a good idea for any long-distance flyer to do the same.

The Argonne National Laboratory has developed an effective program to overcome jet lag that has been adopted by the U.S. Army Rapid Deployment Forces and many Fortune 500 executives. The Argonne anti–jet-lag diet uses certain types of foods and calculated exposure to natural and artificial light to adjust the body's internal time clock. The specifics can be found in the book *Overcoming Jet Lag*, by Dr. Charles F. Ehret and Lynne Waller (published by Berkley Books). While it's available in most airport book stalls, for maximum benefit you really need to purchase it in advance of your departure.

Combat jet lag.

Exercise

The Europeans are ahead of the Americans in recognizing the value of exercise in combating jet lag. Take a Lufthansa flight, and about halfway to Europe, the aisles are full of people striding up and down like cross-country skiers. Isometric exercises, a process of tightening and relaxing your muscles, can be performed discreetly in your seat. These exercises help you to loosen stiff joints and keep muscles toned, while raising your heart rate and increasing the supply of oxygen to your blood.

Keep moving while aloft.

The free booklet *Fitness in the Chair* describes a series of in-flight isometric exercises designed by German Sports Federation president Juergen Palm. To get a copy, send a self-addressed, business-size envelope (unstamped) to Dept. UX12, Lufthansa German Airlines, 1640 Hempstead Turnpike, East Meadow, NY 11554.

SAS offers a similar booklet, *Exercise in the Chair*, which explains eight exercises designed by the company's medical adviser to keep passengers in condition. Request it from SAS, Box EX, 138-02 Queens Boulevard, Jamaica, NY 11435.

Can You Drink the Water?

This is a question heard around the world. The fact is, even where the water is considered perfectly safe, it's smarter to stick to bottled water, fruit juice, or soft drinks.

Why? First, in many parts of the globe, the water is not palatable. Water sources on the Continent are laden with limestone, and the stuff that comes out of the faucet is so hard that instant tea has been known to refuse to dissolve in it. Second, many stomach upsets have more to do with a change in water than with any amoeba that might dwell in it. (This is especially important to keep in mind when traveling with children.) Third, although the airlines and cruise companies might deny it, the water you get on an airplane or cruise ship can be contaminated in storage. Finally, there really are regions of the world where the water is unsafe. Despite all the jokes about "Montezuma's revenge," amoebic dysentery and diarrhea are no laughing matters. Be safe rather than sorry.

Be safe rather than sorry.

It's a simple matter to purchase drinking water when traveling. Nearly every produce stand or grocery store stocks Evian, Panna, or other bottled waters, although you may have to experiment to find one that tastes like what you drink at home. Panna is even available in a soft, treated cardboard container for easy storage and disposal.

Before You Leave Home

Despite your best efforts, you may become ill on a trip. Before you leave home, ask your doctor to help

---

If your travels take you to areas where the water is unsafe, stick to these rules:

1. Drink ONLY boiled or chemically treated water (most U.S. camping-supply stores and drugstores carry water-purification tablets, such as Halazone), or canned or bottled beverages.

2. Do not use ice in your drinks.

3. Brush your teeth using treated or bottled water.

4. Wash your hands often.

5. Eat foods that have been thoroughly cooked and are still hot.

6. Do not eat fruit that somebody else has peeled or prepared.

Don't Leave Home Without Them

you prepare a list of medications that you can take with you in case you become ill and can't get medical assistance right away.

Medications you ought to ask about include these:

- Pepto-Bismol™ (liquid and tablets) Note: Physicians suggest that travelers take four tablets a day to prevent diarrhea; doing so, they say, will cut in half your chances of becoming ill. This regimen should be limited to three weeks, however.

- the prescription drugs Bactrin, Septra, or doxy-cycline (for severe attacks of diarrhea)

- a sodium/sugar mixture and potassium pills, to replace minerals lost from your body

- a mild sedative

Minor Ailments

A word of advice from a seasoned traveler: never leave minor ailments untreated when you're traveling. Chances are they'll only get worse.

A FINAL WORD

If thumbing through this book has given you the itch to set out on your own for foreign climes, it has accomplished the purpose for which it was written. No other occupation outside the travel industry itself offers the opportunities and incentives for travel that teaching affords us.

There is a world of travel waiting for you! *Why not do it?* Whether your tastes run to mountain climbing or lounging at four-star hotels, you can tailor a vacation to fit your dreams. As this book has shown, it doesn't have to be expensive. You can even find travel opportunities that pay *you*. The major ingredients of a great trip are your imagination, a little research, a lot of planning, and the resolve to go ahead and do it. So—why not do it? *Bon voyage!*

Appendix 1

ABSOLUTELY INDISPENSABLE BOOKS AND PAMPHLETS: AN ANNOTATED LIST

U.S. and Worldwide Travel Accommodations Guide. Lists clean, comfortable facilities at more than 650 universities in the U.S., Canada, and overseas where you can find accommodations for $12 to $24 per day. Also included: low-cost YMCA lodging centers; farms, cottages, and inns; discount cruises; and travel opportunities for teachers. Available from Campus Travel Service, P.O. Box 5007, Laguna Beach, CA 92652. Single copy $11.95 plus $1.05 for first-class mail.

Bree, Loris G. *State-by-State Guide to Budget Motels.* St. Paul, MN: MarLor Press, 1988. Lists the best budget motels and independent inns in the U.S. and Canada (priced under $40 per night double, $19.95 single). Itemizes discounts and special rates and provides directions from the freeway.

Lanier, Pamela. *The Complete Guide to Bed & Breakfasts, Inns, & Guesthouses.* Santa Fe, NM: John Muir Publications, 1988. You'll find listings for more than 4,800 North American bed-and-breakfast accommodations and inns, as well as reservation services for 15,000 private guest houses in this informative book.

Directory of English-Speaking Physicians throughout the World. Available from the International Association for Medical Assistance to Travelers (IAMAT), 417 Center St., Lewiston, NY 14092, 716-754-4883. Although when last we heard this directory was free, it would be nice to include a donation in your request, since IAMAT is a nonprofit organization.

116

International Health-Care Service Travelers Guide. Complete information on obtaining health care while abroad. Order from 440 E. 69th St., New York, NY 10021, 212-746-5454, Ext. 61601. Cost: $4.50.

Fischer, Theodore. *Cheap/Smart Travel.* New York: M. Evans and Company Inc., 1987. A complete sourcebook of cheap or free travel, entertainment, and accommodations.

Michelin Green Guides or *Baedaker's Guides.* Thorough descriptions of the history, culture, and tourist attractions of individual countries or major cities of Europe. These books contain absolutely *everything* about sights to see, admission prices, and transportation routes. Not always available overseas.

Michelin Red Guides. The best guides to European hotels, pensions, gasthauses, and inns money can buy. Complete listings of all the accommodations at every price level. A must for the footloose, independent traveler.

Berlitz Pocket-Sized Phrase Books. Available in more than twenty languages. Pick one up for the language of the country you will be visiting—when you get stuck asking directions, you can open the book and point to the phrase you need.

Cohen, Marjorie Adolf. *Work, Study, Travel Abroad.* New York: St. Martin's Press, 1987. Comprehensive information on study-abroad programs, internships, and traineeships; programs that explore the language and culture of a country; and long-term overseas employment. A separate section on teaching is included. Published under the auspices of the Council on International Educational Exchange.

American Students and Teachers Abroad (stock number 1780–01377). For a copy of this pamphlet on studying, working, and teaching abroad, published by the Department of Health and Human Resources, send $1 to Superintendent of Documents, U.S. Government Printing Office, Washington, D.C.

National Directory of Free Tourist Attractions. This directory lists the addresses, telephone numbers, and hours of operation of more than 700 attractions in the U.S., Puerto Rico, and the District of Columbia. Order it from Pilot Books, 103 Cooper St., Babylon, NY 11702; cost: $3.95.

Free Attractions, USA and *Free Campgrounds, USA.* These detailed guides give listings for more than 4,000 free campgrounds, with directions on how to find them. Available for $10.95, plus $1 postage, from Van Meer Publications, Box 1289, Clearwater, FL 33517.

Appendix 2

STATE AND NATIONAL TOURIST OFFICES

United States

Alabama Bureau of Publicity and Information 532 S. Perry St. Montgomery, AL 36104	205-252-2262 800-252-2262
Alaska Division of Tourism Pouch E. 445 Juneau, AK 99811	907-465-2010
Arizona Office of Tourism 3507 North Central Avenue Phoenix, AZ 85012	602-255-3618
Arkansas Department of Parks and Tourism 1 Capitol Mall Little Rock, AR 72201	800-482-8999 (in AR) 800-643-8383
California Department of Economic and Business Affairs Office of Tourism 1030 13th St., Suite 200 Sacramento, CA 95815	916-322-1396
Colorado Division of Commerce and Development Office of Tourism 5500 South Syracuse Circle, Suite 267 Englewood, CO 80111	303-779-1067

Connecticut Department of Economic Development   203-566-3948
Tourism Division
210 Washington St.
Hartford, CT 06106

Delaware State Travel Service   800-282-8667 (in DE)
99 Kings Highway, P.O. Box 1401   800-441-8846
Dover, DE 19903

District of Columbia   202-789-7000
Washington Area Convention and Visitors Assn.
1575 I St., Suite 250
Washington, D.C. 20005

Florida Department of Commerce   904-487-1462
Division of Tourism
126 Van Buren St.
Tallahassee, FL 32301

Georgia Tourist Division   404-656-3590
Dept. of Industry and Trade
P.O. Box 1776
Atlanta, GA 30301

Hawaii Visitors Bureau   808-923-1811
2270 Kalakaua Ave.
Honolulu, HI 96815

Idaho Division of Economic and Community Affairs   800-635-7820
Visitor Information
State Capitol Building, Rm. 108
Boise, ID 83270

Illinois Tourism Information Center   312-793-2094
100 W. Randolph St.
State of Illinois Bldg.
Chicago, IL 60601

Indiana Tourism, Development Division   317-232-8860
1 North Capitol Ave., Suite 700
Indianapolis, IN 46204-2243

Iowa Visitor and Tourism Division   515-281-3210
600 East Court Ave., Suite A
Des Moines, IA 50309

Kansas Travel and Tourism Division   913-296-2009
503 Kansas Ave.
Topeka, KS 66603

Kentucky Travel and Development   800-225-8747
Department of Tourism
Capitol Plaza Tower
Frankfort, KY 40601

Louisiana Office of Tourism
P.O. Box 44291
Baton Rouge, LA 70804

800-231-4730
504-925-3860

Maine Publicity Bureau
97 Winthrop St.
Hallowell, ME 04347

207-289-2423

Maryland Office of Tourist Development
45 Calvert St.
Annapolis, MD 21401

301-269-2686

Massachusetts Division of Tourism
Department of Commerce and Development
100 Cambridge St.
Boston, MA 02202

617-727-3201

Michigan Travel Bureau
Dept. of Commerce
P.O. Box 30226
Lansing, MI 48909

517-373-1195
800-248-5700
800-292-2520 (in MI)

Minnesota Office of Tourism
240 Bremer Bldg.
419 North Robert St.
St. Paul, MN 55101

612-296-5029
800-328-1461
800-652-9747 (in MN)

Mississippi Dept. of Economic Development
Division of Tourism
P.O. Box 849
Jackson, MS 39205

601-359-3414
800-647-2290

Missouri Division of Tourism
308 East High St.
P.O. Box 1055
Jefferson City, MO 65102

314-751-4133

Montana Travel Promotion Bureau
Dept. of Highways
1424 Ninth Ave.
Helena, MT 59620

800-548-3390
406-444-2654 (in MT)

Nebraska Division of Travel and Tourism
P.O. Box 94666
301 Centennial Mall South
Lincoln, NE 68509

402-471-3796
800-228-4307

Nevada Commission on Tourism
Capitol Complex, Suite 207
Carson City, NV 89701

702-885-4322

New Hampshire Office of Vacation Travel
P.O. Box 856
Concord, NH 03301

603-271-2343

New Jersey Division of Travel and Tourism   609-292-2470
P.O. Box CN 826
Trenton, NJ 08625

New Mexico
Economic Development and Tourism Department   505-827-6230
Travel Division   800-545-2040
Bataan Memorial Building, Room 130
Santa Fe, NM 87503

New York Division of Tourism   518-474-4116
State Dept. of Commerce
1 Commerce Plaza
Albany, NY 12245

New York City Convention and Visitors Bureau   212-397-8222
2 Columbus Circle
New York, NY 10019

North Carolina Travel and Tourism Division   919-733-4171
430 North Salisbury St.   800-472-2100 (in NC)
Raleigh, NC 27611   800-438-4404

North Dakota Tourism Promotion Division   701-224-2525
Liberty Memorial Building   800-472-2100 (in ND)
State Capitol Grounds   800-437-2077
Bismarck, ND 58505

Ohio Office of Travel and Tourism   800-282-5393
P.O. Box 1001
Columbus, OH 43216

Oklahoma Tourism Promotion Division   405-521-2409
500 Will Rogers Building
Oklahoma City, OK 73105

Oregon Economic Development   800-547-7842
Tourism Division   800-233-3306 (in OR)
595 Cottage St., Northeast
Salem, OR 97310

Pennsylvania Department of Commerce   800-233-7366
Bureau of Travel Development
416 Forum Building
Harrisburg, PA 17120

Rhode Island Department of Economic Development 401-277-2601
Division of Tourism
7 Jackson Walkway
Providence, RI 02903

South Carolina Department of Parks, Recreation and Tourism 803-758-8570
1205 Pendleton St., Suite 110
Columbia, SC 29201

South Dakota Division of Tourism   800-843-1930
P.O. Box 1000   800-952-2217 (in SD)
Pierre, SD 57501

Tennessee Department of Tourist Development   615-741-2158
P.O. Box 23170
Nashville, TN 37202

Texas Travel and Information Division   512-475-2028
Department of Highways and Public Transportation
P.O. Box 5064
Austin, TX 78763

Utah Travel Council   801-533-5681
Council Hall, Capitol Hill
Salt Lake City, UT 84114

Vermont Travel Division   802-828-3236
134 State St.
Montpelier, VT 05602

Virginia Division of Tourism   804-786-2051
202 North Ninth St., Suite 500
Richmond, VA 23219

Washington Commerce and Economic Development   800-541-9274
Tourism Division   800-541-9274 (in WA)
General Administration Bldg., Room G3
Olympia, WA 98504

West Virginia Travel Development   304-348-2286
Building 6, Room 564   800-624-9110
State Capitol
Charleston, WV 25305

Wisconsin Department of Development   608-266-2161
Division of Tourism
123 West Washington Ave.
Madison, WI 53707

Wyoming Travel Commission   307-777-7777
I-25 at College   800-443-2784
Cheyenne, WY 82002

Nearby Countries (main offices)

Tourism Canada   212-757-4917
1251 Avenue of the Americas
New York, NY 10020

Mexican National Tourist Council   212-755-7212
405 Park Ave.
New York, NY 10022

Caribbean Tourist Association   212-682-0435
20 East 46th St.
New York, NY 10017

Aruba Tourist Board   212-246-3030
1270 Avenue of the Americas
New York, NY 10020

Bahama Tourist Office   212-757-1611
10 Columbus Circle, Suite 16601   800-327-0787
New York, NY 10019

Barbados Board of Tourism   212-986-6516
800 Second Ave.
New York, NY 10017

Bermuda Department of Tourism   212-397-7700
630 Fifth Ave.   800-223-6106
New York, NY 10111

Cayman Islands Dept. of Tourism   212-682-5582
420 Lexington Ave.
New York, NY 10017

Curaçao Tourist Board   212-751-8266
400 Madison Ave., Suite 311
New York, NY 10017

Haiti Tourist Bureau   212-757-3517
1270 Avenue of the Americas, Suite 508
New York, NY 10020

Jamaica Tourist Board   212-688-7650
2 Dag Hammarskjöld Plaza
New York, NY 10017

Puerto Rico Tourism Co.   212-541-6630
1290 Avenue of the Americas
New York, NY 10104

U.S. Virgin Islands Division of Tourism   212-582-4520
1270 Avenue of the Americas
New York, NY 10020

Central and South America

Argentina Consulate General   212-397-1400
12 West 56th St.
New York, NY 10019

Brazilian Tourist Authority   212-286-9600
60 East 42nd St., Suite 1336
New York, NY 10023

Consulate General, Chile   212-688-0151
866 United Nations Plaza
New York, NY 10017

Colombian Government Tourist Office   212-688-0151
140 East 57th St.
New York, NY 10022

Costa Rica Tourist Office   212-245-6370
630 Fifth Ave.
New York, NY 10111

Consulate General, Ecuador   212-683-7355
18 E. 41st St., Room 1800
New York, NY 10017

Peru National Tourist Office   212-969-4020
489 Fifth Ave., Room 3001
New York, NY 10017

Venezuelan Government Tourist and Information Center   212-355-1101
7 E. 51st St.
New York, NY 10022

Europe

Austrian National Tourist Office   212-944-6880
500 Fifth Ave.
New York, NY 10110

Belgian National Tourist Office   212-758-8130
745 Fifth Ave.
New York, NY 10151

Cyprus Tourist Organization   212-686-6016
13 East 40th St.
New York, NY 10016

Cedok Czechoslovakian Travel Bureau   212-689-9720
10 East 40th St.
New York, NY 10016

Danish Tourist Board   212-949-2333
655 Third Ave.
New York, NY 10017

Finnish Tourist Board   212-949-2333
655 Third Ave.
New York, NY 10017

French Government Tourist Office   212-757-1125
610 Fifth Ave.
New York, NY 10017

Embassy of German Democratic Republic (East Germany)   202-232-3134
1717 Massachusetts Ave., N.W.
Washington, D.C. 20036

German National Tourist Office (West Germany)   212-308-3300
747 Third Ave.
New York, NY 10017

Greek National Tourist Organization   212-421-5777
645 Fifth Ave.
New York, NY 10022

Hungarian Travel Bureau (IBUSZ)   212-582-7412
630 Fifth Ave., Suite 520
New York, NY 10111

Iceland Tourist Board   212-949-2333
655 Third Ave.
New York, NY 10017

Irish Tourist Board   212-418-0800
757 Third Ave.
New York, NY 10017

Italian Government Travel Office   212-245-4822
630 Fifth Ave.
New York, NY 10111

Luxembourg National Tourist Office   212-370-9850
801 Second Ave.
New York, NY 10017

Consulate of Malta   212-725-2345
249 East 35th St.
New York, NY 10022

Monaco Government Tourist Office   212-759-5227
845 Third Ave.
New York, NY 10022

Netherlands National Tourist Office   212-223-8141
576 Fifth Ave.
New York, NY 10036

Norwegian National Tourist Office   212-949-2333
655 Third Ave.
New York, NY 10017

Polish National Tourist Office   212-391-0844
500 Fifth Ave.
New York, NY 10110

Portuguese National Tourist Office   212-354-4403
548 Fifth Ave.
New York, NY 10036

Romanian National Tourist Office   212-697-6971
573 Third Ave.
New York, NY 10016

Spanish National Tourist Office   212-759-8822
665 Fifth Ave.
New York, NY 10022

Swedish Tourist Board   212-949-2333
655 Third Ave.
New York, NY 10017

Appendix 2   *125*

Swiss National Tourist Office
608 Fifth Ave.
New York, NY 10020   212-757-5944

Turkish Tourism and Information Office   212-687-2194
821 United Nations Plaza
New York, NY 10017

British Tourist Authority   212-581-4700
40 West 57th St.
New York, NY 10019

Intourist (U.S.S.R.)   212-757-4127
630 Fifth Ave.
New York, NY 10111

Yugoslav State Tourist Office   212-757-2801
630 Fifth Ave.
New York, NY 10111

Africa/Middle East

Egyptian Government Tourist Office   212-246-6960
630 Fifth Ave.
New York, NY 10111

Israel Government Tourist Office   212-560-0650
Empire State Building
350 Fifth Ave.
New York, NY 10118

Kenya Tourist Office   212-486-1300
424 Madison Ave.
New York, NY 10017

Moroccan National Tourist Office   212-557-2520
20 East 46th St., Suite 503
New York, NY 10017

South African Tourism Board   212-838-8841
737 Third Ave.
New York, NY 10017

South Pacific

Australian Tourist Commission   212-489-7550
489 Fifth Ave.
New York, NY 10017

New Zealand Travel Commission   212-586-0060
630 Fifth Ave.
New York, NY 10111

Tahiti Tourist Development Board
B.P. 65
Papeete, Tahiti
French Polynesia

Asia

China National Tourist Office   212-867-0271
60 East 42nd St., Suite 465
New York, NY 10165

Hong Kong Tourist Association   212-869-5008
548 Fifth Ave.
New York, NY 10036

Government of India Tourist Office   212-586-4901
30 Rockefeller Plaza
New York, NY 10112

Indonesian Tourist Promotion Center   212-879-0600
Consulate General
5 East 68th St.
New York, NY 10021

Japan National Tourist Office   212-757-5640
630 Fifth Ave.
New York, NY 10111

Korea National Tourism Corporation   212-688-7543
460 Park Ave., Suite 400
New York, NY 10022

Macao Tourist Information Bureau   212-581-7465
608 Fifth Ave., Suite 309
New York, NY 10020

Nepal Consulate General   212-370-4188
820 Second Ave., Suite 1200
New York, NY 10017

Singapore Tourist Promotion Board   212-687-0385
342 Madison Ave.
New York, NY 10173

Ceylon Tourist Board [Sri Lanka]   212-935-0369
609 Fifth Ave., Suite 714
New York, NY 10017

Taiwan Visitors Association   212-466-0691
1 World Trade Center, Suite 8855
New York, NY 10048

Tourism Authority of Thailand   212-432-0433
5 World Trade Center, Suite 2449
New York, NY 10048

Born in England, Sunni Bloyd has taught reading in six states and West Germany, where a two-year stay provided many opportunities for travel throughout Europe and the Middle East. In addition to leading shopping tours to lesser-known locales, Ms. Bloyd has written many travel articles for newspapers, including *The Stars and Stripes*.

Ms. Bloyd retired from teaching in 1988 to devote her full time to nonfiction writing and has won numerous awards. Her first book *Endangered Species*, was published in the fall of 1989.